THE COMING OF THE FRIARS

BENN'S ESSEX LIBRARY

Edited by Edward G. Hawke, M.A. (Oxon.)

F'cap. 8vo.   Cloth, gilt back, 3s. 6d. each net.

BENN'S ESSEX LIBRARY

Edited by Edward G. Hawke, M.A.

THE REV.
AUGUSTUS JESSOPP, D.D.

THE COMING OF THE
FRIARS

LONDON: ERNEST BENN LTD.

Bouverie House, Fleet Street.

First Edition		.	.	.	.	.	1888
Second Impression							1888
Third	,,	.	.	.	.	.	1888
Fourth	,,	.	.	.	.	.	1890
Fifth	,,	.	.	.	.	.	1892
Sixth	,,	.	.	.	.	.	1892
Seventh	,,	.	.	.	.	.	1895
Eighth	,,	.	.	.	.	.	1896
Ninth	,,	.	.	.	.	.	1898
Tenth	,,	.	.	.	.	.	1899
Eleventh	,,	.	.	.	.	.	1901
Twelfth	,,	.	.	.	.	.	1902
Thirteenth	,,	.	.	.	.	.	1905
Fourteenth	,,	.	.	.	.	.	1906
Fifteenth	,,	.	.	.	.	.	1907
Sixteenth	,,	.	.	.	.	.	1910
Seventeenth	,,	.	.	.	.	.	1913
Eighteenth	,,	.	.	.	.	.	1917
Nineteenth	,,	.	.	.	.	.	1922
Twentieth	,,	.	.	.	.	.	1926
Twenty-first Impression (Essex Library)							1930

To

MY FRIEND AND SOMETIME TUTOR,

FRANCIS WHALLEY HARPER,

CANON OF YORK,

I OFFER THIS VOLUME AS A TOKEN OF MY GRATITUDE.

[These Essays have appeared at various times in " The Nineteenth Century," and are now printed with some alterations, corrections, and additions.]

CONTENTS.

I.

THE COMING OF THE FRIARS.

Sweet St. Francis of Assisi, would that he were here again !
—*Lord Tennyson*

WHEN King Richard of England, whom men call the Lion-hearted, was wasting his time at Messina, after his boisterous fashion, in the winter of 1190, he heard of the fame of Abbot Joachim, and sent for that renowned personage, that he might hear from his own lips the words of prophecy and their interpretation.

Around the personality of Joachim there has gathered no small amount of *mythus*. He was, it appears, the inventor of that mystical method of Hermeneutics which has in our time received the name of " the year-day theory," and which, though now abandoned for the most part by sane men, has still some devout and superstitious advocates in the school of Dr. Cumming and kindred visionaries.

Abbot Joachim proclaimed that a stupendous catastrophe was at hand. Opening the Book of the

Revelation of St. John he read, pondered, and interpreted. A divine illumination opened out to him the dark things that were written in the sacred pages. The unenlightened could make nothing of " a time, times, and half a time " [1]; to them the terrors of the 1,260 days [2] were an insoluble enigma long since given up as hopeless, whose answer would come only at the Day of Judgment. Abbot Joachim declared that the key to the mystery had been to him revealed. What could " a time, times, and half a time " mean, but three years and a half ? What could a year mean in the divine economy but the *lunar* year of 360 days ? for was not the moon the symbol of the Church of God ? What were those 1,260 days but the sum of the days of three years and a half ? Moreover, as it had been with the prophet Ezekiel, to whom it was said, " I have appointed thee a day for a year," so it must needs be with other seers who saw the visions of God. To them the " day " was not as our brief prosaic day—to them too had been "appointed a day for a year." The " time, times, and half a time " were the 1,260 days, and these were 1,260 years, and the stupendous catastrophe, the battle of Armageddon, the reign of Antichrist, the new heavens and the new earth, the slaughter and the resurrection of the two heavenly witnesses, were at hand. Eleven

[1] Dan. xii. 7.   [2] Rev. xi. 3.

hundred and ninety years had passed away of those 1,260. "Hear, O heavens, and give ear, O earth," said Joachim; "Antichrist is already born, yea born in the city of Rome!"

Though King Richard, in the strange interview of which contemporary historians have left us a curious narrative, exhibited much more of the spirit of the scoffer than of the convert, and evidently had no faith in Abbott Joachim's theories and his mission, it was otherwise with the world at large. At the close of the twelfth century a very general belief, the result of a true instinct, pervaded all classes that European society was passing through a tremendous crisis, that the dawn of a new era, or, as they phrased it, "the end of all things" was at hand.

The Abbot Joachim was only the spokesman of his age who was lucky enough to get a hearing. He spoke a language that was a jargon of rhapsody, but he spoke vaguely of terrors, and perils, and earthquakes, and thunderings, the day of wrath; and because he spoke so darkly men listened all the more eagerly, for there was a vague anticipation of the breaking up of the great waters, and that things that had been heretofore could not continue as they were.

Verily when the thirteenth century opened, the times were evil, and no hope seemed anywhere on the horizon. The grasp of the infidel was tightened

upon the Holy City, and what little force there ever
had been among the rabble of Crusaders was gone
now; the truculent ruffianism that pretended to be
animated by the crusading spirit showed its real
character in the hideous atrocities for which Simon
de Montfort is answerable, and in the unparalleled
enormities of the sack of Constantinople in 1204.
For ten years (1198–1208) through the length and
breadth of Germany there was ceaseless and sanguinary conflict. In the great Italian towns party
warfare, never hesitating to resort to every kind of
crime, had long been chronic. The history of Sicily
is one long record of cruelty, tyranny, and wrong—
committed, suffered, or revenged. Over the whole
continent of Europe people seem to have had no
homes; the merchant, the student, the soldier, the
ecclesiastic were always on the move. Young men
made no difficulty in crossing the Alps to attend
lectures at Bologna, or crossing the Channel to or
from Oxford and Paris. The soldier or the scholar
was equally a free-lance, ready to take service where-
ever it offered, and to settle wherever there was
dread to win or money to save. No one trusted in
the stability of anything.[1]

To a thoughtful man watching the signs of the

---

[1] M. Jusserand's beautiful book, "La Vie Nomade," was
not published till 1884, *i.e.,* a year after this essay appeared.

times, it may well have seemed that the hope for the future of civilization—the hope for any future, whether of art, science, or religion—lay in the steady growth of the towns. It might be that the barrier of the Alps would always limit the influence of Italian cities to Italy and the islands of the Mediterranean; but for the great towns of what is now Belgium and Germany what part might not be left for them to play in the history of the world? In England the towns were as yet insignificant communities compared with such mighty aggregates of population as were to be found in Bruges, Antwerp, or Cologne; but even the English towns *were* communities, and they were beginning to assert themselves somewhat loudly while clinging to their chartered rights with jealous tenacity. Those rights, however, were eminently exclusive and selfish in their character. The chartered towns were ruled in all cases by an oligarchy.[1] The increase in the population brought wealth to a class, the class of privileged traders, associated into guilds, who kept their several *mysteries* to themselves by vigilant measures of protection. Outside the well-guarded defences which these trades-unions constructed, there were the masses—hewers of wood and drawers of water—standing to the skilled artizan of the thirteenth century almost precisely in the same relation as the bricklayer's labourer does to the

[1] Stubbs, "Constitutional History," vol. i. § 131.

mason in our own time. The *sediment* of the town population in the Middle Ages was a dense slough of stagnant misery, squalor, famine, loathsome disease, and dull despair, such as the worst slums of London, Paris, or Liverpool know nothing of. When we hear of the mortality among the townsmen during the periodical outbreaks of pestilence or famine, horror suggests that we should dismiss as incredible such stories as the imagination shrinks from dwelling on. What greatly added to the dreary wretchedness of the lower order in the towns was the fact that the ever-increasing throngs of beggars, outlaws, and ruffian runaways were simply left to shift for themselves. The civil authorities took no account of them as long as they quietly rotted and died ; and, what was still more dreadful, the whole machinery of the Church polity had been formed and was adapted to deal with entirely different conditions of society from those which had now arisen.

The idea of the parish priest taking the oversight of his flock, and ministering to each member as the shepherd of the people, is a grand one, but it is an idea which can be realized, and then only approximately, in the village community. In the towns of the Middle Ages the parochial system, except as a *civil* institution, had broken down.

The other idea, of men and women weary of the

hard struggle with sin, and fleeing from the wrath to come, joining together to give themselves up to the higher life, out of the reach of temptation and safe from the witcheries of Mammon,—that too was a grand idea, and not unfrequently it had been carried out grandly. But the monk was nothing and did nothing for the townsman; he fled away to his solitude; the rapture of silent adoration was his joy and exceeding great reward; his nights and days might be spent in praise and prayer, sometimes in study and research, sometimes in battling with the powers of darkness and ignorance, sometimes in throwing himself heart and soul into art which it was easy to persuade himself he was doing only for the glory of God; but all this must go on far away from the busy haunts of men, certainly not within earshot of the multitude. Moreover the monk was, by birth, education, and sympathy, one with the upper classes. What were the rabble to him?[1] In return the townsmen hated him cordially, as a supercilious aristocrat and Pharisee, with the guile and greed of the Scribe and lawyer superadded.

Upon the townsmen—whatever it may have been among the countrymen—the ministers of religion

---

[1] The 20th Article of the Assize of Clarendon is very significant : " Prohibet dominus rex ne monachi . . . recipiant *aliquem de minuto populo in monachum*, vel canonicum vel fratrem," &c.—Stubbs, " Benedict Abbas," pref. p. cliv.

exercised the smallest possible *restraint.* Nay! it was only too evident that the bonds of ecclesiastical discipline which had so often exercised a salutary check upon the unruly had become seriously relaxed of late, both in town and country; they had been put to too great a strain and had snapped. By the suicidal methods of Excommunication and Interdict all ranks were schooled into doing without the rites of religion, the baptism of their children, or the blessing upon the marriage union. In the meantime it was notorious that even in high places there were instances not a few of Christians who had denied the faith and had given themselves up to strange beliefs, of which the creed of the Moslem was not the worst. Men must have received with a smile the doctrine that Marriage was a Sacrament when everybody knew that, among the upper classes at least, the bonds of matrimony were soluble almost at pleasure.[1] It seems hardly worth while to notice

---

[1] Eleanor of Aquitaine, consort of Henry II., had been divorced by Louis VII. of France. Constance of Brittany, mother of Arthur—Shakespeare's idealized Constance—left her husband, Ranulph, Earl of Chester, to unite herself with Guy of Flanders. Conrad of Montferat divorced the daughter of Isaac Angelus, Emperor of Constantinople, to marry Isabella, daughter of Amalric, King of Jerusalem, the bride repudiating her husband Henfrid of Thouars. Philip II. of France married the sister of the King of Denmark one day and divorced her the next; then married a German lady, left her, and returned

that the observance of Sunday was almost universally neglected, or that sermons had become so rare that when Eustace, Abbot of Flai, preached in various places in England in 1200, miracles were said to have ensued as the ordinary effects of his eloquence. Earnestness in such an age seemed in itself miraculous. Here and there men and women, hungering and thirsting after righteousness, raised their sobbing prayer to heaven that the Lord would shortly accomplish the number of his elect and hasten his coming, and Abbot Joachim's dreams were talked of and his vague mutterings made the sanguine hope for better days. Among those mutterings had there not been a speech of the two heavenly witnesses who were to do—ah! what were they not to do? And these heavenly witnesses, who were they? When and where would they appear?

Eight years before King Richard was in Sicily a child had been born in the thriving town of Assisi, thirteen miles from Perugia, who was destined to be one of the great movers of the world. Giovanni Bernardone was the son of a wealthy merchant at Assisi, and from all that appears an only child. He was from infancy intended for a mercantile career,

to the repudiated Dane. King John in 1189 divorced Hawisia, Countess of Gloucester, and took Isabella of Angoulême to wife, but how little he cared to be faithful to the one or the other the chronicles disdain to ask.

nor does he seem to have felt any dislike to it. One story—and it is as probable as the other—accounts for his name Francesco by assuring us that he earned it by his unusual familiarity with the French language, acquired during his residence in France while managing his father's business. The new name clung to him; the old baptismal name was dropped; posterity has almost forgotten that it was ever imposed. From the mass of tradition and personal recollections that have come down to us from so many different sources it is not always easy to decide when we are dealing with pure invention of pious fraud, and when with mere exaggeration of actual fact, but it scarcely admits of doubt that the young merchant of Assisi was engaged in trade and commerce till his twenty-fourth year, living in the main as others live, but perhaps early conspicuous for aiming at a loftier ideal than that of his everyday associates, and characterized by the devout and ardent temperament essential to the religious reformer. It was in the year 1206 that he became a changed man. He fell ill—he lay at Death's door. From the languor and delirium he recovered but slowly—when he did recover old things had passed away; behold! all things had become new. From this time Giovanni Bernardone passes out of sight, and from the ashes of a dead past, from the seed which has withered that the new life might germinate and fructify, Francis—why grudge to call him *Saint* Francis ?—of Assisi rises.

Very early the young man had shown a taste for Church restoration. The material fabric of the houses of God in the land could not but exhibit the decay of living faith ; the churches were falling into ruins. The little chapel of St. Mary and the Angels at Assisi was in a scandalous condition of decay. It troubled the heart of the young pietist profoundly to see the Christian church squalid and tottering to its fall while within sight of it was the Roman temple in which men had worshipped the idols. There it stood, as it had stood for a thousand years —as it stands to this day. Oh, shame ! that Christian men should build so slightly while the heathen built so strongly !

To the little squalid ruin St. Francis came time and again, and poured out his heart, perplexed and sad ; and there, we are told, God met him and a voice said, " Go, and build my church again." It was a "thought beyond his thought," and with the straightforward simplicity of his nature he accepted the message in its literal sense and at once set about obeying it as he understood it.

He began by giving all he could lay his hands on to provide funds for the work. His own resources exhausted, he applied for contributions to all who came in his way. His father became alarmed at his son's excessive liberality and the consequences that might ensue from his strange recklessness; it is even said that he turned him out of doors; it seems that the commercial partnership was cancelled: it is certain that the son was compelled to make some great renunciation of wealth, and that his private means were seriously restricted. That a man of business should be blind to the preciousness of money was a sufficient proof then, as now, that he must be mad.

O ye wary men of the world, bristling with the shrewdest of maxims, bursting with the lessons of experience, ye of the cool heads and the cold grey eyes, ye whom the statesman loves, and the tradesman trusts, cautious, sagacious, prudent; when the rumbling of the earthquake tells us that the foundations of the earth are out of course, we must look for deliverance to other than you! A grain of enthusiasm is of mightier force than a million tons of wisdom such as yours; then when the hour of the great upheaval has arrived, and things can no longer be kept going!

"Build up my church!" said the voice again to this gushing emaciated fanatic in the second-rate Italian town, this dismal bankrupt of twenty-

four years of age, "of lamentably low extraction,"
whom no University claimed as her own, and
whom the learned pundits pitied. At last he
understood the profounder meaning of the words.
It was no temple made with hands, but the *living*
Church that needed raising. The dust of corruption
must be swept away, the dry bones be stirred; the
breath of the divine Spirit blow and reanimate them.
Did not the voice mean that ? What remained but
to obey ?

In his journeyings through France it is hardly
possible that St. Francis should not have heard of
the poor men of Lyons whose peculiar tenets at this
time were arousing very general attention. It is not
improbable that he may have fallen in with one of
those translations of the New Testament into the
vernacular executed by Stephen de Emsa at the
expense of Peter Waldo, and through his means
widely circulated among all classes.[1] Be it as it
may, the words addressed by our Lord to the
seventy, when he sent them forth to preach the
kingdom of heaven, seemed to St. Francis to be
written in letters of flame. They haunted him
waking and sleeping. "The lust of gain in the

[1] See "Facts and Documents Illustrative of the History,
Doctrine, and Rites, of the Ancient Albigenses and Waldenses,"
by the Rev. S. R. Maitland, London, 8vo., 1832, p. 127 *et seq.*

spirit of Cain!" what had it done for the world or
the Church but saturate the one and the other with
sordid greed? Mere wealth had not added to the
sum of human happiness. Nay, misery was growing; kings fought, and the people bled at every
pore. Merchants reared their palaces, and the
masses were perishing. Where riches increased,
there pride and ungodliness were rampant. What
had corrupted the monks, whose lives should be so
pure and exemplary? What but their vast possessions, bringing with them luxury and the paralysis
of devotion and of all lofty endeavour? It was
openly maintained that the original Benedictine
Rule could not be kept now as of yore. One
attempt after another to bring back the old monastic
discipline had failed deplorably. The Cluniac revival had been followed by the Cluniac laxity,
splendour, and ostentation. The Cistercians, who
for a generation had been the sour puritans of the
cloister, had become the most potent religious corporation in Europe; but theirs was the power of the
purse now. Where had the old strictness and the
old fervour gone? Each man was lusting for all
that was not his own; but free alms, where were
they? and pity for the sad, and reverence for the
stricken, and tenderness and sympathy? "O gentle
Jesus, where art Thou? and is there no love of Thee

anywhere, nor any love for Thy lost sheep, Thou crucified Saviour of men?"

.   .   .   .   .   .

Knocking at his heart—not merely buzzing in his brain—the words kept smiting him, "Provide neither gold nor silver nor brass in your purses, neither scrip for your journey, neither two coats, nor yet staves, for the workman is worthy of his meat!" Once men had changed the face of the world with no other equipment. Faith then had removed mountains. Why not again? He threw away his staff and shoes; he went forth with literally a single garment; he was girt with a common rope round his loins. He no more doubted of his mission, he no more feared for the morrow than he feared for the young ravens that he loved and spake to in an ecstasy of joy.

Henceforth there was "not a bird upon the tree but half forgave his being human;" the flowers of the field looked out at him with special greetings, the wolf of the mountains met him with no fierce glare in his eye. Great men smiled at the craze of the monomaniac. Old men shook their grey heads and remembered that they themselves had been young and foolish. Practical men would not waste their words upon the folly of the thing. Rich men, serenely confident of their position, affirmed that they knew of only one who could overcome the world—to wit, the veritable hero, he who holds the purse-strings. St. Francis did not speak to these. "Oh, ye miserable, helpless, and despairing; ye who find yourselves so unutterably forlorn—so very, very far astray; ye lost souls whom Satan has bound through the long weary years; ye of the broken hearts, bowed down and crushed; ye with your wasted bodies loathsome to every sense, to whom life is torture and whom death will not deliver; ye whose very nearness by the wayside makes the traveller as he passes shudder with uncontrollable horror lest your breath should light upon his garments, look! I am poor as you—I am one of yourselves. Christ, the very Christ of God, has sent me with a message to you. Listen!"

It is observable that we never hear of St. Francis that he was a sermon-maker. He had received no clerical or even academical training. Up to 1207 he had not even a license to preach. It was only after this that he was—and apparently without desiring it —ordained a deacon. In its first beginnings the Franciscan movement was essentially moral, not theological, still less intellectual. The absence of anything like dogma in the sermons of the early Minorites was their characteristic. One is tempted to say it was a mere accident that these men were not sectaries, so little in common had they with the ecclesiastics of the time, so entirely did they live and labour among the laity of whom they were and with whom they so profoundly sympathized.

The secret of the overwhelming, the irresistible attraction which St. Francis exercised is to be found in his matchless simplicity, in his sublime self-surrender. He removed mountains because he believed intensely in the infinite power of *mere goodness.* While from the writhing millions all over Europe—the millions ignorant, neglected, plague-stricken, despairing—an inarticulate wail was going up to God, St. Francis made it articulate. Then he boldly proclaimed: "God has heard your cry! It meant this and that. I am sent to you with the good God's answer." There was less than a step between accepting him as the interpreter of their vague yearnings and embracing him as the ambassador of Heaven to themselves.

St. Francis was hardly twenty-eight years old when he set out for Rome, to lay himself at the feet of the great Pope Innocent the Third, and to ask from him some formal recognition. The pontiff, so the story goes, was walking in the garden of the Lateran when the momentous meeting took place. Startled by the sudden apparition of an emaciated young man, bareheaded, shoeless, half-clad, but—for all his gentleness—a beggar who would take no denial, Innocent hesitated. It was but for a brief hour, the next he was won.

Francis returned to Assisi with the Papal sanction for what was, probably, a draught of his afterwards famous "Rule." He was met by the whole city, who received him with a frenzy of excitement. By this time his enthusiasm had kindled that of eleven other young men, all now aglow with the same divine fire. A twelfth soon was added—he, moreover, a layman of gentle blood and of knightly rank. All these had surrendered their claim to everything in the shape of property, and had resolved to follow their great leader's example by stripping themselves of all worldly possessions, and suffering the loss of all things. They were beggars—literally barefooted beggars. The love of money was the root of all evil. They would not touch the accursed thing lest they should be defiled—no, not with the tips of their fingers. "Ye cannot serve God and Mammon."

Beggars they were, but they were brethren — *Fratres* (*Frères*). We in England have got to call them *Friars*. Francis was never known in his lifetime as anything higher than *Brother Francis*, and his community he insisted should be called the community of the lesser brethren—*Fratres Minores*—for none could be or should be *less* than they. Abbots and Priors, he would have none of them. " He that will be chief among you," he said, in Christ's own words, " let him be your servant." The highest official among the *Minorites* was the *Minister*, the elect of all, the servant of all, and if not humble enough to serve, not fit to rule.

People talk of " Monks and Friars " as if these were convertible terms. The truth is that the difference between the Monks and the Friars was almost one of kind. The Monk was supposed never to leave his cloister. The Friar in St. Francis' first intention had no cloister to leave. Even when he had where to lay his head, his life-work was not to save his own soul, but first and foremost to save the bodies and souls of others. The Monk had nothing to do with ministering to others. At best his business was to be the salt of the earth, and it behoved him to be much more upon his guard that the salt should not lose his savour, than that the earth should be sweetened. The Friar was an itinerant evangelist, always on the move. He was a preacher of righteousness. He lifted up his voice against sin and wrong. "Save yourselves from this untoward generation!" he cried ; "save yourselves from the wrath to come." The Monk, as has been said, was an aristocrat. The Friar belonged to the great unwashed !

Without the loss of a day the new apostles of

poverty, of pity, of an all-embracing love, went forth
by two and two to build up the ruined Church of God.
Theology they were, from anything that appears,
sublimely ignorant of.   Except that they were masters of every phrase and word in the Gospels, their
stock in trade was scarcely more than that of an
average candidate for Anglican orders ; but to each
and all of them Christ was simply *everything*.   If
ever men have preached Christ, these men did ;
Christ, nothing but Christ, the Alpha and the Omega,
the first and the last, the beginning and the end.
They had no system, they had no views, they com-
bated no opinions, they took no side.   Let the dia-
lecticians dispute about this nice distinction or that.
There *could* be no doubt that Christ had died and
risen, and was alive for evermore.   There was no place
for controversy or opinions when here was a mere
simple, indisputable, but most awful fact.   Did you
want to wrangle about the aspect of the fact, the
evidence, the what not ?   St. Francis had no mission
to argue with you.   " The pearl of great price—will
you have it or not ?   Whether or not, there are
millions sighing for it, crying for it, dying for it.   To
the poor at any rate the Gospel shall be preached
now as of old."

To the poor by the poor.   Those masses, those
dreadful masses, crawling, sweltering in the foul

hovels, in many a southern town with never a roof
to cover them, huddling in groups under a dry arch,
alive with vermin ; gibbering *cretins* with the ghastly
wens ; lepers by the hundred, too shocking for
mothers to gaze at, and therefore driven forth to
curse and howl in the lazar-house outside the walls,
there stretching out their bony hands to clutch the
frightened almsgiver's dole, or, failing that, to pick
up shreds of offal from the heaps of garbage—to
these St. Francis came.

More wonderful still!—to these outcasts came those
other twelve, so utterly had their leader's sublime
self-surrender communicated itself to his converts.
" We are come," they said, " to live among you and
be your servants, and wash your sores, and make
your lot less hard than it is. We only want to do as
Christ bids us do. We are beggars too, and we too
have not where to lay our heads. Christ sent us to
you. Yes. Christ the crucified, whose we are, and
whose you are. Be not wroth with us, we will help
you if we can."

As they spoke, so they lived. They *were* less than
the least, as St. Francis told them they must strive
to be. Incredulous cynicism was put to silence. It
was wonderful, it was inexplicable, it was disgusting,
it was anything you please ; but where there were
outcasts, lepers, pariahs, there, there were these

penniless Minorites tending the miserable sufferers with a cheerful look, and not seldom with a merry laugh. As one reads the stories of those earlier Franciscans, one is reminded every now and then of the extravagances of the Salvation Army.

The heroic example set by these men at first startled, and then fascinated the upper classes. While labouring to save the lowest, they took captive the highest. The Brotherhood grew in numbers day by day; as it grew, new problems presented themselves. How to dispose of all the wealth renounced, how to employ the energies of all the crowds of brethren. Hardest of all, what to do with the earnest, highly-trained, and sometimes erudite convert who could not divest himself of the treasures of learning which he had amassed. "Must I part with my books?" said the scholar, with a sinking heart. "Carry nothing with you for your journey!" was the inexorable answer. "Not a Breviary? not even the Psalms of David?" "Get them into your heart of hearts, and provide yourself with a treasure in the heavens. Who ever heard of Christ reading books save when He opened the book in the synagogue, and *then closed* it and went forth to teach the world for ever?"

In 1215 the new Order held its first Chapter at the Church of the Portiuncula. The numbers of the

Brotherhood and the area over which their labours
extended had increased so vastly that it was already
found necessary to nominate Provincial Ministers in
France, Germany, and Spain.

————————————

While these things were going on in Italy, another
notable reformer was vexing his righteous soul in
Spain. St. Dominic was a very different man from
the gentle and romantic young Italian. Of high
birth, which among the haughty Castillians has
always counted for a great deal, he had passed his
boyhood among ecclesiastics and academics. He
was twelve years older than St. Francis. He studied
theology for ten years at the University of Palencia,
and before the twelfth century closed he was an
Augustinian Canon. In 1203, while St. Francis
was still poring over his father's ledgers, Dominic
was associated with the Bishop of Osma in nego-
ciating a marriage for Alphonso the Eighth, king of
Castille. For the next ten years he was more or
less concerned with the hideous atrocities of the
Albigensian war. During that dark period of his
career he was brought every day face to face with
heresy and schism. From infancy he must have
heard those around him talk with a savage intolerance of the Moors of the South and the stubborn

Jews of Toledo nearer home. Now his eyes were open to the perils that beset the Church from sectaries who from within were for casting off her divine authority. Wretches who questioned the very creeds and rejected the Sacraments, yet perversely insisted that they were Christian men and women, with a clearer insight into Gospel mysteries than Bishops and Cardinals or the Holy Father himself. Here was heresy rampant, and immortal souls, all astray, beguiled by evil men and deceivers, "whose word doth eat as doth a canker." Dominic "saw that there was no man, and marvelled that there was no intercessor."

It was not ungodliness that Dominic, in the first instance, determined to war with, but ignorance and error. *These* were to him the monster evils, whose natural fruit was moral corruption. Get rid of them and the depraved heart might be dealt with by-and-by. Dominic stood forth as the determined champion of orthodoxy. "Preach the word in season, out of season; reprove, rebuke, exhort"—that was his panacea. His success at the first was but small. Preachers with the divine fervour, with the gift of utterance, with the power to drive truth home—are rare. They are not to be had for the asking; they are not to be trained in a day. Years passed, but little was achieved.

Dominic was patient. He had, indeed, founded a small religious community of sixteen brethren at St. Ronain, near Toulouse—one of these, we are told, was an Englishman—whose aim and object were to produce an effect through the agency of the pulpit, to confute the heretics and instruct the unlearned. The Order, if it deserved the name, was established on the old lines. A monastery was founded, a local habitation secured. The maintenance of the brotherhood was provided for by a sufficient endowment; the petty cares and anxieties of life were in the main guarded against; but when Innocent the Third gave his formal sanction to the new community, it was given to Dominic and his associates, on the 8th of October, 1215, as to a house of *Augustinian Canons*, who received permission to enjoy in their corporate capacity the endowments which had been bestowed upon them.[1]

In the following July Innocent died, and was at once succeeded by Honorius the Third. Dominic set out for Rome, and on the 22nd of December he received from the new Pope a bare confirmation of what his predecessor had granted, with little more than a passing allusion to the fact that the new

---

[1] So "La Cordaire, vie de S. Dominique" (1872), p. 120. It was, however, a very curious community, as appears from "Ripolli Bullarium Prædicat:" I. i.

B

canons were to be emphatically *Preachers* of the faith. In the autumn of 1217 Dominic turned his back upon Languedoc for ever. He took up his residence at Rome, and at once rose high in the favour of the Pope. His eloquence, his earnestness, his absorbing enthusiasm, his matchless dialectic skill, his perfect scholastic training—all combined to attract precisely those cultured churchmen whose fastidious sense of the fitness of things revolted from the austerities of St. Francis and the enormous demands which the Minorites made upon their converts. While Francis was acting upon the masses from Assisi, Dominic was stirring the dry bones to a new vitality among scholars and ecclesiastics at Rome.

Thus far we have heard little or nothing of poverty among the more highly educated *Friars Preachers*, as they got to be called. That seems to have been quite an afterthought. So far as Dominic may be said to have accepted the Voluntary Principle and, renouncing all endowments, to have thrown himself and his followers for support upon the alms of the faithful, so far he was a disciple of St. Francis. The Champion of Orthodoxy was a convert to the Apostle of Poverty.

How soon the Dominicans gave in their adhesion to the distinctive tenet of the Minorites will never now be known, nor how far St. Francis himself adopted it from others; but a conviction that holiness of life had deteriorated in the Church and the cloister by reason of the excessive wealth of monks and ecclesiastics was prevalent everywhere, and a belief was growing that sanctity was attainable only by those who were ready to part with all their worldly possessions and give to such as needed. Even before St. Francis had applied to Innocent the Third, the poor men of Lyons had come to Rome begging for papal sanction to their missionary plans; they met with little favour, and vanished from the scene. But they too declaimed against endowments —they too were to live on alms. The Gospel of Poverty was " *in the air.*"

In 1219 the Franciscans held their second general Chapter. It was evident that they were taking the world by storm; evident, too, that their astonishing success was due less to their preaching than to their self-denying lives. It was abundantly plain that this vast army of fervent missionaries could live from day to day and work wonders in evangelizing the masses without owning a rood of land, or having anything to depend upon but the perennial stream of bounty which flowed from the gratitude of the converts. If the Preaching Friars were to succeed at such a time as this, they could only hope to do so by exhibiting as sublime a faith as the Minorites displayed to the world. Accordingly, in the very year after the second Chapter of the Franciscans was held at Assisi, a general Chapter of the Dominicans was held at Bologna, and there the profession of poverty was formally adopted, and the renunciation of all means of support, except such as might be offered from day to day, was insisted on. Henceforth the two orders were to labour side by side in magnificent rivalry—mendicants who went forth like Gideon's host with empty pitchers to fight the battles of the Lord, and whose desires, as far as the good things of this world went, were summed up in the simple petition, " Give us this day our daily bread ! "

———————

Thus far the friars had scarcely been heard of in England. The Dominicans—trained men of education, addressing themselves mainly to the educated classes, and sure of being understood wherever Latin, the universal medium of communication among scholars, was in daily and hourly use—the Dominicans could have little or no difficulty in getting an audience such as they were qualified to address. It was otherwise with the Franciscans. If the world was to be divided between these two great bands, obviously the Minorites' sphere of labour must be mainly among the lowest, that of the Preaching Friars among the cultured classes.

When the Minorites preached among Italians or Frenchmen they were received with tumultuous welcome. They spoke the language of the people; and in the vulgar speech of the people—rugged, plastic, and reckless of grammar—the message came as glad tidings of great joy. When they tried the same method in Germany, we are told, they signally failed. The gift of tongues, alas! had ceased. That, at any rate, was denied, even to such faith as theirs. They were met with ridicule. The rabble of Cologne or Bremen, hoarsely grumbling out their grating gutturals, were not to be moved by the most impassioned pleading of angels in human form, soft though their voices might be, and musical their tones. "Ach Himmel! was sagt er?" growled one. And peradventure some well-meaning interpreter replied: "Zu suchen und selig zu machen." When the Italian tried to repeat the words his utterance, not his faith, collapsed! The German-speaking people must wait till a door should be opened. Must England wait too? Yes! For the Franciscan missionaries England too must wait a little while.

But England was exactly the land for the Dominican to turn to. Unhappy England! Dominic was born in the same year that Thomas à Becket was murdered in Canterbury Cathedral; Francis in the year before the judgment of the Most High began to fall upon the guilty king and his accursed progeny. Since then everything seemed to have gone wrong. The last six years of Henry the Second's reign were years of piteous misery, shame, and bitterness. His two elder sons died in arms against their father, the one childless, the other, Geoffrey, with a baby boy never destined to arrive at manhood. The two younger ones were Richard and John. History has no story more sad than that of the wretched king, hard at death's door, compelled to submit to the ferocious vindictiveness of the one son, and turning his face to the wall with a broken heart when he discovered the hateful treachery of the other. Ten years after this Richard died childless, and King John was crowned—the falsest, meanest, worst, and wickedest king that ever sat upon the throne of

England. And now John himself was dead; and
" Woe to thee, O land, when thy king is a child!"
for Henry the Third was crowned, a boy just nine
years old.

For eight years England had lain under the
terrible interdict; for most of the time only a
single bishop had remained in England. John had
small need to tax the people: he lived upon the
plunder of bishops and abbots. The churches were
desolate; the worship of God in large districts
almost came to an end. Only in the Cistercian
monasteries, and in them only for a time, and to a
very limited extent, were the rites of religion continued. It is hardly conceivable that the places of
those clergy who died during the eight years of the
interdict were supplied by fresh ordinations; and
some excuse may have been found for the outrageous
demands of the Pope to present to English benefices
in the fact that many cures must have been vacant,
and the supply of qualified Englishmen to succeed
them had fallen short.

Strange to say, in the midst of all this religious
famine, and while the Church was being ruthlessly
pillaged and her ministers put to rebuke, there was
more intellectual activity in the country than had
existed for centuries. The schools at Oxford were
attracting students from far and near; and when, in

consequence of the disgraceful murder of three *clerics* in 1209, apparently at the instance of King John, the whole body of masters and scholars dispersed— some to Cambridge, others to Reading—it is said their number amounted to 3,000. These were for the most part youths hardly as old as the under-graduates in a Scotch university in our own time ; but there was evidently an ample supply of competent teachers, or the reputation of Oxford could not have been maintained.

It was during the year after the Chapter of the Dominicans held at Bologna in 1220, that the first brethren of the order arrived in England. They were under the direction of one Gilbert de Fraxineto, who was accompanied by twelve associates. They landed early in August, probably at Dover. They were at once received with cordiality by Archbishop Langton, who put their powers to the test by commanding one of their number to preach before him. The Primate took them into his favour, and sent them on their way. On the 10th of August they were preaching in London, and on the 15th they appeared in Oxford, and were welcomed as the bringers-in of new things. Their success was un-equivocal. We hardly hear of their arrival before we learn that they were well established in their school and surrounded by eager disciples.

Be it remembered that any systematic training of young men to serve as evangelists—any attempt to educate them directly as preachers well furnished with arguments to confute the erring, and carefully taught to practise the graces of oratory—had never been made in England. These Dominicans were already the Sophists of their age, masters of dialectic methods then in vogue, whereby disputation had been raised to the dignity of a science. Then a scholar was looked upon as a mere pretender who could not maintain a *thesis* against all comers before a crowded audience of sharp-witted critics and eager partisans, not too nice in their expressions of dissent or approval. The exercises still kept up for the Doctor's degree in Divinity at Oxford and Cambridge are but the shadow of what was a reality in the past. Whether we have not lost much in the discontinuance of the old *Acts* and *Apponencies*, which at least assured that a young man should be required to stand up before a public audience to defend the reasonableness of his opinions, may fairly be doubted. The aim of the Dominican teachers was to turn out trained preachers furnished with all tricks of dialectic fence, and practised to extempore speaking on the most momentous subjects. Unfortunately the historian, when he has told us of the arrival of his brethren, leaves us in the dark as

B 2

to all their early struggles and difficulties, and passes on to other matters with which we are less concerned. What would we not give to know the history, say during only twenty years, of the labours of the Preaching Friars in England? Alas! it seems never to have been written. We are only told enough to awaken curiousity and disappoint it.

Happily, of the early labours of the Franciscan friars in England much fuller details have reached us, though the very existence of the records in which they were handed down was known to very few, and the wonderful story had been forgotten for centuries when the appearance of the "Monumenta Franciscana" in the series of chronicles published under direction of the Master of the Rolls in 1858 may be said to have marked an event in literature. If the late Mr. Brewer had done no more than bring to light the remarkable series of documents which that volume contains, he would have won for himself the lasting gratitude of all seekers after truth.

The Dominicans had been settled in Oxford just two years when the first band of Franciscan brethren landed in England on the 11th of September, 1224. They landed penniless; their passage over had been paid by the monks of Fécamp; they numbered in all nine persons, five were laymen, four were clerics. Of the latter three were Englishmen, the fourth was an

Italian, Agnellus of Pisa by name. Agnellus had been some time previously destined by St. Francis as the first *Minister* for the province of England, not improbably because he had some familiarity with our language. He was about thirty years of age, and as yet only in deacon's orders. Indeed, of the whole company *only one was a priest*, a man of middle age who had made his mark and was famous as a preacher of rare gifts and deep earnestness. He was a Norfolk man born, Richard of Ingworth by name and presumably a priest of the diocese of Norwich. Of the five laymen one was a Lombard, who may have had some kinsfolk and friends in London, where he was allowed to remain as warden for some years, and one, Lawrence of Beauvais, was a personal and intimate friend of St. Francis, who on his death-bed gave him the habit which he himself had worn.

The whole party were hospitably entertained for two days at the Priory of the Holy Trinity at Canterbury. Then brother Richard Ingworth, with another Richard—a Devonshire youth conspicuous for his ascetic fervour and devotion, but only old enough to be admitted to minor orders—set out for London, accompanied by the Lombard and another foreigner, leaving behind him Agnellus and the rest, among them William of Esseby, the third Englishman, enthusiastic and ardent as the others, but a mere youth and as yet a novice. He, too, I conjecture to have been a Norfolk or Suffolk man, whose birth-place, *Ashby*, in the East Anglian dialect, would be pronounced nearly as it is written in Eccleston's manuscript. It was arranged that Richard Ingworth should lose no time in trying to secure some place where they might all lay their heads, and from whence as a centre they might begin the great work they had in hand. The Canterbury party were received into the Priest's House and allowed to remain for a while. Soon they received permission to sleep in a building used as a school during the day-time, and while the boys were being taught the poor friars huddled together in a small room adjoining, where they were confined as if they had been prisoners. When the scholars went home the friars crept out, lit a fire and sat round it, boiled their porridge, and mixed their small beer, sour and thick as we are told it was, with water to make it go further, and each contributed some word of edification to the general stock, brought forward some homely illustration which might serve to brighten the next sermon when it should be preached, or told a pleasant tale, thought out during the day—a story with a moral. Of the five left behind at Canterbury it is to be observed that no one of them was qualified as yet to preach in the vernacular. William of Esseby was too young for the pulpit, though he became a very effective preacher in a few years. He was, however, doing good service as interpreter, and doubtless as teacher of English to the rest.

Before long the cheerfulness, self-denial, and devout bearing of the little company at Canterbury gained for them the warm support and friendship of all classes. They had a very hard time of it. Sometimes a kind soul would bring them actually a dish of meat, sometimes even a bottle of wine, but as a rule their fare was bread—made up into *twists*, we hear, when it was specially excellent—wheat-bread, wholesome and palatable; but, alas, sometimes barley-bread, washed down with beer too sour to drink undiluted with water. Alexander, the master of the Priest's House at Canterbury, soon after gave them a piece of ground and built them a temporary chapel, but when he was for presenting them with the building, he was told that they might not possess houses and lands, and the property was thereupon made over to the corporation of Canterbury to hold in honourable trust for their use, the friars *borrowing* it of the town. Simon Langton too, Archdeacon of Canterbury, the primate's brother, stood their friend, and one or two people of influence among the laity, as Sir Henry de Sandwich, a

wealthy Kentish gentleman, and a lady whom
Eccleston calls a "noble countess," one Inclusa de
Baginton, warmly supported them and liberally supplied their necessities. It is worthy of notice that
at Canterbury their first friends were among the
wealthy, *i.e.*, those among whom a command of
English was not necessary.

While Agnellus and his brethren were waiting
patiently at Canterbury, Ingworth and young Richard
of Devon with the two Italians had made their way
to London and had been received with enthusiasm.
Their first entertainers were the Dominican friars who,
though they had been only two years before them,
yet had already got for themselves a house, in which
they were able to entertain the new-comers for a
fortnight. At the end of that time they hired a plot
of ground in Cornhill of John Travers, the Sheriff of
London, and there they built for themselves a house,
such as it was. Their cells were constructed like
sheep-cotes, mere wattels with mouldy hay or straw
between them. Their fare was of the meanest, but
they gained in estimation every day. In their
humble quarters at Cornhill they remained preaching,
visiting, nursing, begging their bread, but always
gay and busy, till the summer of 1225, when a certain John Iwyn—again a name suspiciously like the
phonetic representative of the common Norfolk name

of *Ewing*—a mercer and citizen, offered them a more spacious and comfortable dwelling in the parish of St. Nicholas. As their brethren at Canterbury had done, so did they ; they refused all houses and lands, and the house was made over to the corporation of London for their use. Not long after the worthy citizen assumed the Franciscan habit and renounced the world, to embrace poverty.

In the autumn of 1225 Ingworth and the younger Richard left London, Agnellus taking their place. He had not been idle at Canterbury, and his success in making converts had been remarkable. At Canterbury and London the Minorites had secured for themselves a firm footing. The Universities were next invaded. The two Richards reached Oxford about October, 1225, and as before were received with great cordiality by the Dominicans, and hospitably entertained for eight days. Before a week was out they had got the loan of a house or hall in the parish of St. Ebbs, and had started lectures and secured a large following. Here young Esseby joined them, sent on it seems by Agnellus from London to assist in the work ; a year or so older than when he first landed, and having shown in that time unmistakable signs of great capacity and entire devotion to the work. Esseby was quite able to stand alone.

Once more the two Richards moved on to North-
ampton, where an " opening from the Lord " seemed
to have presented itself.   By this time the whole
country was on the tip-toe of expectation and crowds
of all classes had given in their adhesion to the new
missionaries.   No ! it was *not* grandeur or riches or
honour or learning that were wanted above all things
—not these, but Goodness, Meekness, Simplicity,
and Truth.   The love of money *was* the root of all
evil.   The Minorites were right.   When men with
a divine fervour proclaim a truth, or even half a
truth, which the world has forgotten, there is never
any lack of enthusiasm in its acceptance.   In five
years from their first arrival the Friars had established themselves in almost every considerable town
in England, and where one order settled the other
came soon after, the two orders in their first beginning co-operating cordially.   It was only when their
faith and zeal began to wax cold that jealousy broke
forth into bitter antagonism.

In no part of England were the Franciscans received
with more enthusiasm than in Norfolk.   They appear
to have established themselves at Lynn, Yarmouth,
and Norwich in 1226.   Clergy and laity, rich and poor,
united in offering to them a ready homage.   To this
day a certain grudging provincialism is observable in
the East Anglian character.   A Norfolk man dis-

trusts the settler from "the Shires," who comes in with new-fangled reforms. To this day the home of wisdom is supposed to be in the East. When it was understood that the virtual leader of this astonishing religious revival was a Norfolk man, the joy and pride of Norfolk knew no bounds. Nothing was too much to do for their own hero. But when it became known that Ingworth had been welcomed with open arms by Robert Grosseteste, the foremost scholar in Oxford—he a Suffolk man—and that Grosseteste's friend, Roger de Weseham, was their warm supporter, son of a Norfolk yeoman, whose brethren were to be seen any day in Lynn market—the ovation that the Franciscans met with was unparalleled. There was a general rush by some of the best men of the county into the order.

Already St. Francis had found it necessary to include in the fraternity a class of recognized associates who may be described as the *unattached*. These were the *Tertiaries*—laymen who were not prepared to embrace the vows of poverty and to surrender their all—but well-wishers pledged to support the Minorites, and to co-operate with them when called upon, showing their good-will sometimes in visiting the sick and needy, sometimes in engaging in the work of teaching, or accompanying the preachers when advisable, and bound by their engagement to set an example of sobriety and seriousness in their dress and manners.

Up to this time the word *religious* had been applied only to such as were inmates of a cloister. Now the truth dawned upon men that it was possible to live the higher life even while pursuing one's ordinary vocation in the busy world. The tone of social morality must have gained enormously by the dissemination of this new doctrine, and its acceptance among high and low. It became the fashion in the upper classes to enrol oneself among the Tertiaries, and every new enrolment was an important accession to the stability, and, indeed, to the material resources of the Minorites; and when, apparently within a few days of one another—no less than five gentlemen of knightly rank, of whom at least one, Sir Giles de Merc, had only recently been employed as an envoy by the king to his brother Richard in Gascony, and another, Sir Henry de Walpole, was amongst the most considerable and wealthy men in the eastern counties, Henry the Third spoke out his mind and showed that he was not too well-pleased. Really these friars were going on too fast—turning men's heads! At Lynn the Franciscans were specially fortunate in their warden, whose austerity of life, gentle manners, and profoundly sympathetic temperament obtained for him unbounded influence.

Among others Alexander de Bassingbourne [1]—seneschal of Lynn for Pandulph, Bishop of Norwich, and, as such, a personage of importance, became his convert and joined the new order; but the number of Norfolk clergy and scholars who actually became friars must have been very large indeed; they were quite the picked men among the Franciscans in England. Of the first eighteen masters of Franciscan schools at Cambridge, at least ten were Norfolk men, while of the first five Divinity readers at Oxford whose names have been recorded, after those of Grosseteste and Roger de Weseham, four were unmistakably East Anglians. No one familiar with Norfolk topography could fail to be struck by this fact, and the queer spellings of some places, which puzzled even Mr. Brewer, are themselves suggestive. [2]

St. Francis died at Assisi on October 4, 1226. With his death troubles began. Brother Elias, who was chosen to succeed him as Minister General of the Order, had little of the great founder's spirit, and none of his genius. There was unseemly strife and rivalry, and on the Continent it would

[1] The name is again changed into *Bissing*burne by Eccleston, who writes it as he heard it from Norfolk people.

[2] *E.g.*, Turnham represents the Norfolk pronunciation of *Thornham*. Heddele is *Hadleigh*, in Suffolk spelt phonetically; Ravingham is *Raveningham*, Assewelle is *Ashwell* [cf. p. 93, Esseby for Ashby], Sloler is *Sloley*, Leveringfot is *Letheringset*.

appear that the Minorites made but little way. Not so was it in England; there the supply of brethren animated by genuine enthusiasm and burning zeal for the cause they had espoused was unexampled. Perhaps there more than anywhere else such labourers were needed, perhaps too they had a fairer field. Certainly there they were truer to their first principles than elsewhere.

Outside the city walls at Lynn and York and Bristol; in a filthy swamp at Norwich, through which the drainage of the city sluggishly trickled into the river, never a foot lower than its banks; in a mere barn-like structure, with walls of mud, at Shrewsbury, in the " Stinking Alley " in London, the Minorites took up their abode, and there they lived on charity, doing for the lowest the most menial offices, speaking to the poorest the words of hope, preaching to learned and simple such sermons— short, homely, fervent, and emotional—as the world had not heard for many a day. How could such evangelists fail to win their way? Before Henry III.'s reign was half over the predominance of the Franciscans over Oxford was almost supreme. At Cambridge their influence was less dominant only because at Cambridge there was no commanding genius like Robert Grosseteste to favour and support them.

St. Francis's hatred of book-learning was the one sentiment that he never was able to inspire among his followers. Almost from the first scholars, students, and men of learning were attracted by the irresistible charm of his wonderful moral persuasiveness; they gave in their adherence to him in a vague hope that by contact with his surpassing holiness virtue would go out of him, and that somehow the divine goodness which he magnified as the one thing needful would be communicated to them and supply that which was lacking in themselves; but they could not bring themselves to believe that culture and holiness were incompatible or that nearness to God was possible only to those who were ignorant and uninstructed. We should have expected learning among the Dominicans, but very soon the English Franciscans became the most learned body in Europe, and that character they never lost till the suppression of the monasteries swept them out of the land. Before Edward I. came to the throne, in less than fifty years after Richard Ingworth and his little band landed at Dover, Robert Kilwarby, a Franciscan friar, had been chosen Archbishop of Canterbury, and Bonaventura, the General of the Order, had refused the Archbishopric of York. In 1281 Jerome of Ascoli, Bonaventura's successor as General, was elected Pope, assuming the name of Nicholas IV.

Meanwhile such giants as Alexander Hales and Roger Bacon and Duns Scotus among the Minorites —all Englishmen be it remembered—and Thomas Aquinas and Albertus Magnus among the Dominicans, had given to intellectual life that amazing lift into a higher region of thought, speculation, and inquiry which prepared the way for greater things by-and-by. It was at Assisi that Cimabue and Giotto received their most sublime inspiration and did their very best, breathing the air that St. Francis himself had breathed and listening day by day to traditions and memories of the saint, told peradventure by one or another who had seen him alive or even touched his garments in their childhood. It may even be that there Dante watched Giotto at his work while the painter got the poet's face by heart.

To write the history of the Mendicant Orders in England would be a task beyond my capacity, but no man can hope to understand the successes or the failures of any great party in Church or State until he has arrived at some comprehension, not only of the objects which it set itself to achieve, but of its *modus operandi* at the outset of its career.

The Friars were a great party in the Church, organized with a definite object, and pledged to carry out that object in simple reliance upon what we now call the *Voluntary Principle*. St. Francis saw, and saw much more clearly than even we of the nineteenth century see it, that the Parochial system is admirable, is a perfect system for the village, that it is unsuited for the town, that in the towns the attempt to work it had ended in a miserable and scandalous failure. The Friars came as helpers of the poor town clergy, just when those clergy had begun to give up their task as hopeless. They came as missionaries to those whom the town clergy had got to regard as mere *pariahs*. They came to strengthen the weak hands, and to labour in a new field. *St. Francis was the John Wesley of the thirteenth century, whom the Church did not cast out.*

Rome has never been afraid of fanaticism. She has always known how to utilise her enthusiasts fired by a new idea. The Church of England has never known how to deal with a man of genius. From Wicklif to Frederick Robertson, from Bishop Peacock to Dr. Rowland Williams, the clergyman who has been in danger of impressing his personality upon Anglicanism, where he has not been the object of relentless persecution, has at least been regarded with timid suspicion, has been shunned by the prudent men of low degree, and by those of high degree has been—forgotten. In the Church of England there has never been a time when the enthusiast has not been treated as a very *unsafe* man. Rome has found a place for the dreamiest mystic or the noisiest ranter—found a place and found a sphere of useful labour. We, with our insular prejudices, have been sticklers for the narrowest uniformity, and yet we have accepted, as a useful addition to the Creed of Christendom, one article which we have only not formulated because, perhaps, it came to us from a Roman Bishop, the great sage Talleyrand— *Surtout pas trop de zèle!*

The Minorites were the Low Churchmen of the thirteenth century, the Dominicans the severely orthodox, among whom spiritual things were believed to be attainable only through the medium of significant form. Rome knew how to yoke the two together, Xanthos and Balios champing at the bit yet always held well in hand. At the outset the two orders were so deeply impressed by the magnitude of the evils they were to combat that they hardly knew there was anything in which they were at variance. Gradually—yes, and somewhat rapidly—each borrowed something from the other. The Minorites found they could not do without culture; the Dominicans renounced endowments; by-and-by they drew apart into separate camps, and discord proved that the old singleness of purpose and loyalty to a great cause had passed away. Imitators arose. Reformers they all professed to be, improvers of the original idea. Augustinian Friars, Carmelites, Bethlehemites, Bonhommes, and the rest. Friars they all called themselves — all pledged to the Voluntary Principle, all renouncing endowments, all professing to live on alms.

I have called St. Francis the John Wesley of the thirteenth century. The parallels might be drawn out into curious detail, if we compared the later history of the great movements originated by one or the other reformer. The new orders of Friars were to the old ones what the Separatists among the Wesleyan body are to the Old Connexion. They had their grievances, real or imagined, they loudly protested against corruption and abuses, they professed themselves anxious only to go back to first principles. Rome absorbed them all; they became the Church's great army of volunteers, perfectly disciplined, admirably handled; their very jealousies and rivalries turned to good account. When John Wesley offered to the Church of England precisely their successors, we would have no commerce with them; we did our best to turn them into a hostile and invading force.

The Friars were the Evangelizers of the towns in England for 300 years. When the spoliation of the religious houses was decided upon, the Friars were the first upon whom the blow fell—the first and the last.[1] But when their property came to be looked into, there was nothing to rob but the churches in which they worshipped, the libraries in which they studied, and the houses in which they passed their lives. Rob the county hospitals to-morrow through the length and breadth of the land, or make a general scramble for the possessions of the Wesleyan body, and how many broad acres would go to the hammer?

Voluntaryism leaves little for the spoiler.

As with the later history of the Friars in England, so with the corruptions of the Mendicant orders—though they were as great as malice or ignorance may have represented them—I am not concerned That the Minorites of the fourteenth century were very unlike the Minorites of the thirteenth I know; that the other Mendicant orders declined, I cannot doubt—

> What keeps a spirit wholly true
> To that ideal which he bears?
> What record?   Not the sinless years
> That breathed beneath the Syrian blue.

The Rule of St. Francis was a glorious ideal;

[1] The king began with the Franciscan convent of Christ Church, London, in 1532 ; he bestowed the Dominican convent at Norwich upon the corporation of that city on the 25th of June, 1540.

when it came to be carried into practice by creatures of flesh and blood, it proved to be something to dream of, not to live. And yet, even as it was, its effects upon the Church, nay, upon the whole civilized world, were enormous. If, one after another, the Mendicant orders declined, if their zeal grew cold, their simplicity of life faded, and their discipline relaxed; if they became corrupted by that very world which they promised to purify and deliver from the dominion of Mammon—this is only what has happened again and again, what must happen as long as men are men. In every age the prophet has always asked for the unattainable, always pointed to a higher level than human nature could breathe in, always insisted on a measure of self-renunciation which saints in their prayers send forth the soul's lame hands to clutch—in their ecstasy of aspiration hope that they may some day arrive at. But, alas! they reach it—never. And yet the saint and the prophet do not live in vain. They send a thrill of noble emotion through the heart of their generation, and the divine tremor does not soon subside; they gather round them the pure and generous—the lofty souls which are not all of the earth earthy. In such, at any rate, a fire is kindled by the spark that has fallen from the altar. By-and-by it is the fuel that fails: then the old fire, after smouldering for a while, goes out, and by no stirring of the dead embers can you make them flame again. You may cry as loudly as you will, " Pull down the chimney that will not draw, and set up another in its place!" That you may do if you please; another fire you may have, but the new will not be as the old.

II

VILLAGE LIFE SIX HUNDRED YEARS AGO.

"The rude forefathers of the hamlet . . ."

[IN the autumn of 1878, while on a visit at Rougham Hall, Norfolk, the seat of Mr. Charles North, my kind host drew my attention to some large boxes of manuscripts, which he told me nobody knew anything about, but which I was at liberty to ransack to my heart's content. I at once dived into one of the boxes, and then spent half the night in examining some of its treasures. The chest is one of many, constituting in their entirety a complete apparatus for the history of the parish of Rougham from the time of Henry the Third to the present day—so complete that it would be difficult to find in England a collection of documents to compare with it.

The whole parish contains no more than 2,627 acres, of which about thirty acres were not included in the estate slowly piled up by the Yelvertons, and purchased by Roger North in 1690.

Yet the charters and evidences of various kinds which were handed over with this small property, and which date *before* the sixteenth century, count by thousands. The smaller strips of parchment or vellum—for the most part conveyances of land, and having seals attached—have been roughly bound together in volumes, each containing about one hundred documents, and arranged with some regard to chronology, the undated ones being collected into a volume by themselves. I think it almost certain that the arranging of the early charters in their rude covers was carried out before 1500 A.D., and I have a suspicion that they were grouped together by Sir William Yelverton, "the cursed Norfolk Justice" of the Paston Letters, who inherited the estate from his mother in the first half of the fifteenth century.

When Roger North purchased the property the ancient evidences were handed over to him as a matter of course; and there are many notes in his handwriting showing that he found the collection in its present condition, and that he had bestowed much attention upon it. Blomefield seems to have been aware of the existence of the Rougham muniments, but I think he never saw them; and for one hundred and fifty years, at least, they had lain forgotten until they came under my notice. Of this large mass of documents I had copied or abstracted scarcely more than five hundred, and I had not yet got beyond the year 1355. The court rolls, bailiffs' accounts, and early leases, I had hardly looked at when this lecture was delivered.

The following address gives some of the results of my examination of the first series of the Rougham charters. It was delivered in the Public Reading-room of the village of Tittleshall, a parish adjoining Rougham, and was listened to with apparent interest and great attention by an audience of farmers, village tradesmen, mechanics, and labourers. I was careful to avoid naming any place which my audience were not likely to know well; and there is hardly a parish mentioned which is five miles from the lecture-room.

When speaking of "six hundred years," I gave myself roughly a limit of thirty years before and after 1282, and I have rarely gone beyond that limit on one side or the other.

They who are acquainted with Mr. Rogers' "History of Prices" will observe that I have ventured to put forward views, on more points than one, very different from those which he advocates.

Of the value of Mr. Rogers' compilation, and of the statistics which he has tabulated, there can be but one opinion. It is when we come to draw our inferences from such returns as these, and bring to bear upon them the sidelights which further evidence affords, that differences of opinion arise among inquirers. I really know nothing about the Midlands in the Middle Ages; I am disgracefully ignorant of the social condition of the South and West; but the early history of East Anglia, and especially of Norfolk, has for long possessed a fascination for me; and though I am slow to arrive at conclusions, and have a deep distrust of those historians who, for every pair of facts, construct a Trinity of Theories, I feel sure of my ground on some matters, because I have done my best to use all such evidence as has come in my way.]

———————

Few things have struck me more forcibly since I have cast in my lot among country people, than the strange ignorance which they exhibit of the *history of themselves*. I do not allude to those unpleasant secrets which we should be very sorry indeed for our next-door neighbours to be acquainted with, nor to any such matters as our experience or memories of actual facts could bring to our minds; I mean something very much more than that. Men and women are not only the beings they appear to be at any one moment of their lives, they are not single separate atoms like grains of sand. Rather they are like branches or leaves of some great tree, from which they have sprung and on which they have grown, whose life in the past has come at last to them in the present, and without whose deep anchorage in the soil, and its ages of vigour and vitality, not a bud or a spray that is so fresh and healthful now would have had any existence.

Consider for a moment—Who are we, and what do we mean by *Ourselves?* When I meet a ragged, shuffling tramp on the road (and I meet a good many of them in my lonely walks) I often find myself asking the question, " How did that shambling vagabond come to his present condition ? Did his father turn him out of doors ? Did his mother drink ? Did he learn nothing but lying and swearing and thieving when he was a child ? Was his grandfather hanged for some crime, or was his great-grandfather a ruffian killed in a fight ? " And I say to myself, " Though I do not know the truth, yet I am sure that man was helped towards his vagabondism, helped to become an outcast as he is, by the neglect or the wickedness, the crimes or the bad example of his fathers and forefathers on one side or the other; for if he had come of decent people on both sides, people who had been honestly and soberly brought up themselves, as they tried to bring up their children, yonder dirty tramp would not and could not have sunk to his

c

present self, for we and ourselves are what we come to, partly by our own sins and vices, but partly (and much more than some like to believe) by the sins, negligences, and ignorances of those whose blood is in our veins.

My friends, it surely must be worth our while to know much more than most of us do know about *Ourselves.*

Being convinced of this, and believing, moreover, that to most of us nothing on earth is so interesting as that which most concerns ourselves at any period of our existence, I resolved, when I was asked to address you here this evening, that I would try to give you some notion of the kind of life which your fathers led in this parish a long, long time ago, and so help you to understand through what strange changes we have all passed, and what strange stories the walls of our houses, if they could speak, would have to tell, and on what wonderful struggles, and hardships, and dangers, and sorrows yonder church tower of yours has looked down, since, centuries ago, it first rose up, the joy and pride of those whose hands laid stone on stone.

When I came to think over the matter, however, I found that I could not tell you very much that I was sure of about your own parish of Tittleshall, but that it so happened I could tell you something that is new to you about a parish that joins your own; and because what was going on among your close neighbours at any one time would be in the main pretty much what would be going on among your forefathers, in bringing before you the kind of life which people led in the adjoining parish of Rougham six hundred years ago, I should be describing precisely the life which people were leading here in this parish where we are now—people, remember, whose blood is throbbing in the veins of some of you present; for from that dust that lies in your churchyard yonder I make no doubt that some of you have sprung—you whom I am speaking to now.

Six hundred years ago! Yes, it is a long time. Not a man of you can throw his thoughts back to so great a lapse of time. I do not expect it of you; but nevertheless I am going to try to give you a picture of a Norfolk village, and that a village which you all know better than I do, such as it was six hundred years ago.

In those days an ancestor of our gracious Queen, who now wears the crown of England, was king; and the Prince of Wales, whom many of you must have seen in Norfolk, was named *Edward* after this same king. In those days there were the churches standing generally where they stand now. In those days, too, the main roads ran pretty much where they now run; and there was the same sun overhead, and there were clouds, and winds, and floods, and storms, and sunshine; but if you, any of you, could be taken up and dropped down in Tittleshall or Rougham such as they were at the time I speak of, you would feel almost as strange as if you had been suddenly transported to the other end of the world.

The only object that you would at all recognize would be the parish church. That stands where it did, and where it has stood, perhaps, for a thousand years or more; but, at the time we are now concerned with, it looked somewhat different from what it looks now. It had a tower, but that tower was plainer and lower than the present one. The windows, too, were very different; they were smaller and narrower; I think it probable that in some of them there was stained glass, and it is almost certain that the walls were covered with paintings representing scenes from the Bible, and possibly some stories from the lives of the saints, which everybody in those days was familiar with. There was no pulpit and no reading desk. When the parson preached, he preached from the steps of the altar. The altar itself was much more ornamented than now it is. Upon the altar there were always some large wax tapers which were lit on great occasions, and over the altar there hung a small lamp which was kept alight night and day. It was the parson's first duty to look to it in the morning, and his last to trim it at night.

The parish church was too small for the population of Rougham, and the consequence was that it had been found necessary to erect what we should now call a chapel of ease—served, I suppose, by an assistant priest, who would be called a chaplain. I cannot tell you where this chapel stood, but it had a burial-ground of its own.[1]

There was, I think, only one road deserving the name, which passed through Rougham. It ran almost directly north and south from Coxford Abbey to Castle Acre Priory. But do not suppose that a road in those days meant what it does now. To begin with, people in the country never drove about in carriages. In such a place as Rougham, men and women might live all their lives without ever seeing a travelling carriage, whether on four wheels or two.[2] The road was quite unfit for driving on. There were

---

[1] Compare the remarkable regulations of Bishop Woodloke of Winchester (A.D. 1308), illustrative of this. Wilkins' " Conc.," vol. ii. p. 296. By these constitutions every chapel, two miles from the mother church, was bound to have its own burying-ground

[2] It is, however, not improbable that when the Queen came into Norfolk, the eyes of the awe-struck rustics may have been dazzled by even such an astonishing equipage as is figured in Mr. Parker's " Hist. Domestic Architecture," vol. ii. p. 141.

no highway rates. Now and then a roadway got so absolutely impassable, or a bridge over a stream became so dangerous, that people grumbled; and then an order came down from the king to the high sheriff of the county, bidding him see to his road, and the sheriff thereupon taxed the dwellers in the hundred and forced them to put things straight. The village of Rougham in those days was in its general plan not very unlike the present village—that is to say, the church standing where it does, next to the churchyard was the parsonage with a croft attached; and next to that a row of houses inhabited by the principal people of the place, whose names I could give you, and the order of their dwellings, if it were worth while. Each of these houses had some outbuildings—cowsheds, barns, &c., and a small croft fenced round. Opposite these houses was another row facing west, as the others faced east; but these latter houses were apparently occupied by the poorer inhabitants—the smith, the carpenter, and the general shopkeeper, who called himself, and was called by others, the *merchant*. There was one house which appears to have stood apart from the rest and near Wesenham Heath. It probably was encircled by a moat, and approached by a drawbridge, the bridge being drawn up at sunset. It was called the Lyng House, and had been probably built two or three generations back, and now was occupied by a person of some consideration—viz., Thomas Middleton, Archdeacon of Suffolk, and brother of William Middleton, then Bishop of Norwich. This house was on the east side of the road, and the road leading up to it had a name, and was called the Hutgong. In front of the house was something like a small park of 5½ acres inclosed; and next that again, to the south, 4 acres of ploughed land; and behind that again—that is, between it and the village —there was the open heath. Altogether, this property consisted of a house and 26 acres. Archdeacon Middleton bought it on October 6, 1283, and he bought it in conjunction with his brother Elias, who was soon after made seneschal or steward of Lynn for his other brother, the bishop. The two brothers probably used this as their country house, for both of them had their chief occupation elsewhere; but when the bishop died, in 1288, and they became not quite the important people they had been before, they sold the Lyng House to another important person, of whom we shall hear more by-and-by.

The Lyng House, however, was not the great house of Rougham. I am inclined to think *that* stood not far from the spot where Rougham Hall now stands. It was in those days called the Manor House, or the Manor.

And this brings me to a point where I must needs enter into some explanations. Six hundred years ago all the land in England was supposed to belong to the king in the first instance. The king had in former times parcelled it out into tracts of country, some large and some small, and made over these tracts to his great lords, or barons, as they were called. The barons were supposed to hold these tracts, called fiefs, as *tenants* of the king, and in return they were expected to make an acknowledgment to the king in the shape of some *service*, which, though it was not originally a money payment, yet became so eventually, and was always a substantial charge upon the land. These fiefs were often made up of estates in many different shires; and, because it was impossible for the barons to cultivate all their estates themselves, they let them out to *sub-tenants*, who in their turn were bound to render services to the lord of the fief. These sub-tenants were the great men in the several parishes, and became the actual lords of the manors, residing upon the manors, and having each, on their several manors, very large powers for good or evil over the tillers of the soil.

A manor six hundred years ago meant something very different from a manor now. The lord was a petty king. having his subjects very much under his thumb. But his subjects differed greatly in rank and status. In the first place, there were those who were called the free tenants. The free tenants were they who lived in houses of their own and cultivated land of their own, and who made only an annual money payment to the lord of the manor as an acknowledgment of his lordship. The payment was trifling, amounting to some few pence an acre at the most, and a shilling or so, as the case might be, for the house. This was called the *rent*, but it is a very great mistake indeed to represent this as the same thing which we mean by rent now-a-days. It really was almost identical with what we now call in the case of house property, " ground rent," and bore no proportion to the value of the produce that might be raised from the soil which the tenant held. The free tenant was neither a yearly tenant, nor a leaseholder. His holding was, to all intents and purposes, his own —subject, of course, to the payment of the ground rent. But if he wanted to sell out of his holding, the lord of the manor exacted a payment for the privilege. If he died, his heir had to pay for being admitted to his inheritance, and if he died without heirs, the property went back to the lord of the manor, who then, but only then, could raise the ground rent if he pleased, though he rarely did so. So much for the free tenants.

C 2

Besides these were the *villeins* or *villani*, or *natives*, as they were called. The villeins were tillers of the soil, who held land under the lord, and who, besides paying a small money ground rent, were obliged to perform certain arduous services to the lord, such as to plough the lord's land for so many days in the year, to carry his corn in the harvest, to provide a cart on occasion, &c. Of course these burdens pressed very heavily at times, and the services of the villeins were vexatious and irritating under a hard and unscrupulous lord. But there were other serious inconveniences about the condition of the villein or native. Once a villein, always a villein. A man or woman born in villeinage could never shake it off. Nay, they might not even go away from the manor to which they were born, and they might not marry without the lord's license, and for that license they always had to pay. Let a villein be ever so shrewd or enterprising or thrifty, there was no hope for him to change his state, except by the special grace of the lord of the manor.[1] Yes, there *was* one means

---

[1] I do not take account of those who ran away to the corporate towns. I suspect that there were many more cases of this than some writers allow. It was sometimes a serious inconvenience to the lords of manors near such towns as Norwich or Lynn. A notable example may be found in the " Abbrev. Placit.," p. 316 (6°. E. ii. Easter term). It seems that no less than eighteen villeins of the Manor of Cossey were named in a

whereby he could be set free, and that was if he could get a bishop to ordain him. The fact of a man being ordained at once made him a free man, and a knowledge of this fact must have served as a very strong inducement to young people to avail themselves of all the helps in their power to obtain something like an education, and so to qualify themselves for admission to the clerical order and to the rank of free-man.

At Rougham there was a certain Ralph Red, who was one of these villeins under the lord of the manor, a certain William le Butler. Ralph Red had a son Ralph, who I suppose was an intelligent youth, and made the most of his brains. He managed to get ordained about six hundred years ago, and he became a chaplain, perhaps to that very chapel of ease I mentioned before. His father, however, was still a villein, liable to all the villein services, and *belonging* to the manor and the lord, he and all his offspring. Young Ralph did not like it, and at last, getting the money together somehow, he bought his father's freedom, and, observe, with his freedom the freedom of all his father's children too, and the price he paid

mandate to the Sheriff of Norfolk and Suffolk, who were to be taken and reduced to villeinage, and their goods seized. Six of them pleaded that they were citizens of Norwich—the city being about four miles from Cossey.

was twenty marks.[1] That sounds a ridiculously small sum, but I feel pretty sure that six hundred years ago twenty marks would be almost as difficult for a penniless young chaplain to get together as £500 for a penniless young curate to amass now. Of the younger Ralph, who bought his father's freedom, I know little more; but, less than one hundred and fifty years after the elder man received his liberty, a lineal descendant of his became lord of the manor of Rougham, and, though he had no son to carry on his name, he had a daughter who married a learned judge, Sir William Yelverton, Knight of the Bath, whose monument you may still see at Rougham Church, and from whom were descended the Yelvertons, Earls of Sussex, and the present Lord Avonmore, who is a scion of the same stock.

When Ralph Red bought his father's freedom of William le Butler, William gave him an acknowledgment for the money, and a written certificate of the transaction, but he did not sign his name. In those days nobody signed their names, not because they could not write, for I suspect that just as large a proportion of people in England could write well six hundred years ago, as could have done so forty

[1] N.B.—A man could not buy his own freedom, Merewether's "Boroughs," i. 350. Compare too Littleton on "Tenures," p 65, 66.

years ago, but because it was not the fashion to sign one's name. Instead of doing that, everybody who was a free man, and a man of substance, in executing any legal instrument, affixed to it his *seal*, and that stood for his signature. People always carried their seals about with them in a purse or small bag, and it was no uncommon thing for a pickpocket to cut off this bag and run away with the seal, and thus put the owner to very serious inconvenience. This was what actually did happen once to William le Butler's father-in-law. He was a certain Sir Richard Bell-house, and he lived at North Tuddenham, near Dereham. Sir Richard was High Sheriff for the counties of Norfolk and Suffolk in 1291, and his duties brought him into court on January 25th of that year, before one of the Judges at Westminster. I suppose the court was crowded, and in the crowd some rogue cut off Sir Richard's purse, and made off with his seal. I never heard that he got it back again.[1]

And now I must return to the point from which I wandered when I began to speak of the free tenants and the " villeins." William le Butler, who sold old Ralph Red to his own son, the young Ralph, was himself sprung from a family who had held the Manor of Rougham for about a century. His father

[1] Abbreviatio Placit. 284, b.

was Sir Richard le Butler, who died about 1280, leaving behind him one son, our friend William, and three daughters. Unfortunately, William le Butler survived his father only a very short time, and he left no child to succeed him. The result was that the inheritance of the old knight was divided among his daughters, and what had been hitherto a single lordship became three lordships, each of the parceners looking very jealously after his own interest, and striving to make the most of his powers and rights.

Though each of the husbands of Sir Richard le Butler's daughters was a man of substance and influence—yet, when the manor was divided, no one of them was anything like so great a person as the old Sir Richard. In those days, as in our own, there were much richer men in the country than the country gentlemen, and in Rougham at this time there were two very prosperous men who were competing with one another as to which should buy up most land in the parish, and be the great man of the place. The one of these was a gentleman called Peter the Roman, and the other was called Thomas the Lucky. They were both the sons of Rougham people, and it will be necessary to pursue the history of each of them to make you understand how things went in those "good old times."

First let me deal with Peter the Roman. He was

the son of a Rougham lady named Isabella, by an Italian gentleman named Iacomo de Ferentino, or if you like to translate it into English, James of Ferentinum.

How James of Ferentinum got to Rougham and captured one of the Rougham heiresses we shall never know for certain. But we do know that in the days of King Henry, who was the father of King Edward, there was a very large incursion of Italian clergy into England, and that the Pope of Rome got preferment of all kinds for them. In fact, in King Henry's days the Pope had immense power in England, and it looked for a while as if every valuable piece of preferment in the kingdom would be bestowed upon Italians who did not know a word of English, and who often never came near their livings at all. One of these Italian gentlemen, whose name was *John* de Ferentino, was very near being made Bishop of Norwich; [1] he *was* Archdeacon of Norwich, but though the Pope tried to make him bishop, he happily did not succeed in forcing him into the see that time, and John of Ferentinum had to content himself with his archdeaconry and one or two other preferments.

[1] At the death of Thomas de Blunville in 1236. John de Ferentino must have been almost supreme in the diocese. The see was practically vacant for three years.

Our friend at Rougham may have been, and probably was, some kinsman of the archdeacon, and it is just possible that Archdeacon Middleton, who, you remember, bought the Lyng House, may have had, as his predecessor in it, another archdeacon, this John de Ferentino, whose nephew or brother, James, married Miss Isabella de Rucham, and settled down among his wife's kindred. Be that as it may, John de Ferentino had two sons, Peter and Richard, and it appears that their father, not content with such education as Oxford or Cambridge could afford— though at this time Oxford was one of the most renowned universities in Europe—sent his sons to Rome, having an eye to their future advancement; for in King Henry's days a young man that had friends at Rome was much more likely to get on in the world than he who had only friends in the King's Court, and he who wished to push his interests in the Church must look to the Pope, and not to the King of England, as his main support.

When young Peter came back to Rougham, I dare say he brought back with him some new airs and graces from Italy, and I dare say the new fashions made his neighbours open their eyes. They gave the young fellow the name he is known by in the charters, and to the day of his death people called him Peter Romayn, or Peter the Roman. But Peter came back a changed man in more ways than one. He came back a *cleric*. We in England now recognize only three orders of clergy—bishops, priests, and deacons. But six hundred years ago it was very different. In those days a man might be two or three degrees below a deacon, and yet be counted a cleric and belonging to the clergy; and, though Peter Romayn was not priest or deacon, he was a privileged person in many ways, but a very unprivileged person in one way—he might never marry.

It was a hard case for a young man who had taken to the clerical profession without taking to the clerical life, and all the harder because there were old men living whose fathers or grandfathers had known the days when even a Bishop of Norwich was married, and who could tell of many an old country clergyman who had had his wife and children in the parsonage. But now—just six hundred years ago—if a young fellow had once been admitted a member of the clerical body, he was no longer under the protection of the laws of the realm, nor bound by them, but he was under the dominion of another law, commonly known as the Canon Law, which the Pope of Rome had succeeded in imposing upon the clergy; and in accordance with that law, if he took to himself a wife, he was, to all intents and purposes, a ruined man.

But when laws are pitted against human nature, they may be forced upon people by the strong hand of power, but they are sure to be evaded where they are not broken literally; and this law of forbidding clergymen to marry *was* evaded in many ways. Clergymen took to themselves wives, and had families. Again and again their consciences justified them in their course, whatever the Canon Law might forbid or denounce. They married on the sly—if that may be called marriage which neither the Church nor the State recognized as a binding contract, and which was ratified by no formality or ceremony civil or religious: but public opinion was lenient; and where a clergyman was living otherwise a blameless life, his people did not think the worse of him for having a wife and children, however much the Canon Law and certain bigoted people might give the wife a bad name. And so it came to pass that Peter Romayn of Rougham, cleric though he were, lost his heart one fine day to a young lady at Rougham, and marry he would. The young lady's name was Matilda. Her father, though born at Rougham, appears to have gone away from there when very young, and made money somehow at Leicester. He had married a Norfolk lady, one

Agatha of Cringleford; and he seems to have died, leaving his widow and daughter fairly provided for; and they lived in a house at Rougham, which I dare say Richard of Leicester had bought. I have no doubt that young Peter Romayn was a young gentleman of means, and it is clear that Matilda was a very desirable bride. But then Peter *couldn't* marry! How was it to be managed? I think it almost certain that no religious ceremony was performed, but I have no doubt that the two plighted their troth either to each, and that somehow they did become man and wife, if not in the eyes of Canon Law, yet by the sanction of a higher law to which the consciences of honourable men and women appeal against the immoral enactments of human legislation.

Among the charters at Rougham I find eighteen or twenty which were executed by Peter Romayn and Matilda. In no one of them is she called his wife; in all of them it is stipulated that the property shall descend to whomsoever they shall leave it, and in only one instance, and there I believe by a mistake of the scribe, is there any mention of their *lawful* heirs. They buy land and sell it, sometimes separately, more often conjointly, but in all cases the interests of both are kept in view; the charters are witnessed by the principal people in the place, including Sir Richard Butler himself, more than once; and in one of the later charters Peter Romayn, as if to provide against the contingency of his own death, makes over all his property in Rougham without reserve to Matilda, and constitutes her the mistress of it all.[1]

Some year or two after this, Matilda executes her last conveyance, and executes it alone. She sells her whole interest in Rougham—the house in which she lives and all that it contains—lands and ground rents, and everything else, for money down, and we hear of her no more. Did she retire from the world, and find refuge in a nunnery? Did she go away to some other home? Who knows? And what of Peter the Roman? I know little of him, but I suspect the pressure put upon the poor man was too strong for him, and I suspect that somehow, and, let us hope, with much anguish and bitterness of heart—but yet somehow, he was compelled to repudiate the poor woman to whom there is evidence to show he was true and staunch as long as it was possible—and when it was no longer possible I *think* he too turned his back upon the Rougham home, and

---

[1] By the constitutions of Bishop Woodloke, any *legacies* left by a clergyman to his "concubine" were to be handed over to the bishop's official, and distributed to the poor.—Wilkins' "Conc." vol. ii. p. 296 b.

was presented by the Prior of Westacre Monastery to the Rectory of Bodney at the other end of the county, where, let us hope, he died in peace.

It is a curious fact that Peter Romayn was not the only clergyman in Rougham whom we know to have been married. As for Peter Romayn, I believe he was an honourable man according to his light, and as far as any men were honourable in those rough days. But for the other. I do not feel so sure about him.

I said that the two prosperous men in Rougham six hundred years ago were Peter Romayn and Thomas the Lucky, or, as his name appears in the Latin Charters, Thomas Felix. When Archdeacon Middleton gave up living at Rougham, Thomas Felix bought his estate, called the Lyng House; and shortly after he bought another estate, which, in fact, was a manor of its own, and comprehended thirteen free tenants and five villeins; and, as though this were not enough, on September 24, 1292, he took a lease of another manor in Rougham for six years, of one of the daughters of Sir Richard le Butler, whose husband, I suppose, wanted to go elsewhere. Before the lease expired he died, leaving behind him a widow named Sara and three little daughters, the eldest of whom cannot have been more than eight or nine years old. This was in the year 1294. Sara, the widow, was for the time a rich woman, and she made up her mind never to marry again, and she kept her resolve.

When her eldest daughter Alice came to the mature age of fifteen or sixteen, a young man named John of Thrysford wooed and won her. Mistress Alice was by no means a portionless damsel, and Mr. John seems himself to have been a man of substance. How long they were married I know not; but it could not have been more than a year or two, for less than five years after Mr. Felix's death a great event happened, which produced very momentous effects upon Rougham and its inhabitants in more ways than one.

Up to this time there had been a rector at Rougham, and apparently a good rectory-house and some acres of glebe land—how many I cannot say. But the canons of Westacre Priory cast their eyes upon the rectory of Rougham, and they made up their minds they would have it. I dare not stop to explain how the job was managed—that would lead me a great deal too far—but it *was* managed, and accordingly, a year or two after the marriage of little Alice, they got possession of all the tithes and the glebe, and the good rectory-house at Rougham, and they left the parson of the parish with a smaller house on the other side of the road. and *not* contiguous to the church, an allowance of two quarters of wheat and two quarters of barley a year, and certain small dues which might suffice to keep body and soul together but little more.[1]

John of Thyrsford had not been married more than a year or two when he had had enough of it. Whether at the time of his marriage he was already a *cleric*, I cannot tell, but I know that on October 10, 1301, he was a priest, and that on that day he was instituted to the vicarage of Rougham, having been already divorced from poor little Alice. As for Alice —if I understand the case, she never could marry, however much she may have wished it; she had no children to comfort her; she became by-and-by the great lady of Rougham, and there she lived on for nearly fifty years. Her husband, the vicar, lived on too—on what terms of intimacy I am unable to say.

[1] This appears from the following charter, which it seems worth while to quote: "Pateat universis . . . quod nos Robertus de Feletone, Miles, et Hawigia uxor mea concessimus . . . Alicie filie Thome de Rucham . . . Totum ius nostrum . . . in terris . . . dicte Alicie . . . in Rucham, que . . . habuimus de dono et dimissione Johannis filii Roberti de Thyrsforde in Rucham *ante diuorstium* (sic) *inter eundem Johannem et dictam* Aliciam factum . . . Omnia munimenta et scripta que de dicto tenemento habuimus eidem Alicie quiete reddidimus . . . Datum apud Lucham die Dom: prox: post Annunc: B Mar: Virg: Anno R. R. Edw: fit. Reg. Henr: tricessimo tertio" (28 March, 1305).—*Rougham Charter*, No. 157.

The vicar died some ten years before the lady. When old age was creeping on her she made over all her houses and lands in Rougham to feoffees, and I have a suspicion that she went into a nunnery and there died.

In dealing with the two cases of Peter Romayn and John of Thyrsford I have used the term *cleric* more than once. These two men were, at the end of their career at any rate, what we now understand by clergyman; but there were hosts of men six hundred years ago in Norfolk who were *clerics*, and yet who were by no means what we now understand by clergymen. The *clerics* of six hundred years ago comprehended all those whom we now call the professional classes; all, *i.e.*, who lived by their brains, as distinct from those who lived by trade or the labour of their hands.

Six hundred years ago it may be said that there were two kinds of law in England, the one was the law of the land, the other was the law of the Church. The law of the land was hideously cruel and merciless, and the gallows and the pillory, never far from any man's door, were seldom allowed to remain long out of use. The ghastly frequency of the punishment by death tended to make people savage and bloodthirsty.[1] It tended, too, to make men abso-

---

[1] In 1293 a case is recorded of three men, one of them a goldsmith, who had their right hands chopped off in

lutely reckless of consequences when once their passions were roused. " As well be hung for a sheep as a lamb " was a saying that had a grim truth in it. When a violent ruffian knew that if he robbed his host in the night he would be sure to be hung for it, and if he killed him he could be no more than hung, he had nothing to gain by letting him live, and nothing to lose if he cut his throat. Where another knew that by tampering with the coin of the realm he was sure to go to the gallows for it, he might as well make a good fight before he was taken, and murder any one who stood in the way of his escape. Hanging went on at a pace which we cannot conceive, for in those days the criminal law of the land was not, as it is now, a strangely devised machinery for protecting the wrongdoer, but it was an awful and tremendous power for slaying all who were dangerous to the persons or the property of the community.

The law of the Church, on the other hand, was much more lenient. To hurry a man to death with his sins and crimes fresh upon him, to slaughter men wholesale for acts that could not be regarded as enormously wicked, shocked those who had learnt

the middle of the street in London.—" Chron. of Edward I. and Edward II.," vol. i. p. 102. Ed. Stubbs. Rolls Series.

that the Gospel taught such virtues as mercy and longsuffering, and gave men hopes of forgiveness on repentance. The Church set itself against the atrocious mangling, and branding, and hanging that was being dealt out blindly, hastily, and indiscriminately, to every kind of transgressor; and inasmuch as the Church law and the law of the land six hundred years ago were often in conflict, the Church law acted to a great extent as a check upon the shocking ferocity of the criminal code. And this is how the check was exercised.

A man who was a *cleric* was only half amenable to the law of the land. He was a citizen of the realm, and a subject of the king, but he was *more;* he owed allegiance to the Church, and claimed the Church's protection also. Accordingly, whenever a *cleric* got into trouble, and there was only too good cause to believe that if he were brought to his trial he would have a short shrift and no favour, scant justice and the inevitable gallows within twenty-four hours at the longest, he proclaimed himself a *cleric*, and demanded the protection of the Church, and was forthwith handed over to the custody of the ordinary or bishop. The process was a clumsy one, and led, of course, to great abuses, but it had a good side. As a natural and inevitable consequence of such a privilege accorded to a class, there was a very strong inducement to become a member of that class; and as the Church made it easy for any fairly educated man to be admitted at any rate to the lower orders of the ministry, any one who preferred a professional career, or desired to give himself up to a life of study, enrolled himself among the *clerics*, and was henceforth reckoned as belonging to the clergy.

The country swarmed with these *clerics*. Only a small proportion of them ever became ministers of religion; they were lawyers, or even lawyers' clerks; they were secretaries; some few were quacks with nostrums; and these all were just as much *clerics* as the chaplains, who occupied pretty much the same position as our curates do now—clergymen, strictly so called, who were on the look out for employment, and who earned a very precarious livelihood—or the rectors and vicars who were the beneficed clergy, and who were the parsons of parishes occupying almost exactly the same position that they do at this moment, and who were almost exactly in the same social position as they are now. Six hundred years ago there were at least seven of these *clerics* in Rougham, all living in the place at the same time besides John of Thyrsford, the vicar. Five of them were chaplains, two were merely *clerics*. If there were *seven* of these clerical gentlemen whom I happen to have met with in my examination of the Rougham

Charters, there must have been others who were not people of sufficient note to witness the execution of important legal instruments, nor with the means to buy land or houses in the parish. It can hardly be putting the number too high if we allow that there must have been at least ten or a dozen *clerics* of one sort or another in Rougham six hundred years ago.

How did they all get a livelihood? is a question not easy to answer; but there were many ways of picking up a livelihood by these gentlemen. To begin with, they could take an engagement as tutor in a gentleman's family; or they could keep a small school; or earn a trifle by drawing up conveyances, or by keeping the accounts of the lord of the manor. In some cases they acted as private chaplains, getting their victuals for their remuneration, and sometimes they were merely loafing about, and living upon their friends, and taking the place of the country parson if he were sick or past work. Then, too, the smaller monasteries had one or more chaplains, and I suspect that the canons at Castle Acre always would keep two or three chaplains in their pay, and it is not unlikely that as long as Archdeacon Middleton kept on his big house at Rougham he would have a chaplain, who would be attached to the place, and bound to perform the service in the great man's chapel.

But besides the clerics and the chaplains and the rector or vicar, there was another class, the members of which just at this time were playing a very important part indeed in the religious life of the people, and not in the religious life alone; these were the Friars. If the monks looked down upon the parsons, and stole their endowments from them whenever they could, and if in return the parsons hated the monks and regarded them with profound suspicion and jealousy, both parsons and monks were united in their common dislike of the Friars.

Six hundred years ago the Friars had been established in England about sixty years, and they were now by far the most influential Religionists in the country. The Friars, though always stationed in the towns, and by this time occupying large establishments which were built for them in Lynn, Yarmouth, Norwich, and elsewhere, were always acting the part of itinerant preachers, and travelled their circuits on foot, supported by alms. Sometimes the parson lent them the church, sometimes they held a camp meeting in spite of him, and just as often as not they left behind them a feeling of great soreness, irritation, and discontent; but six hundred years ago the preaching of the Friars was an immense and incalculable blessing to the country, and if it had not been for the wonderful reformation wrought by their activity and burning enthusiasm, it is difficult to see what we should have come to or what corruption might have prevailed in Church and State.

When the Friars came into a village, and it was known that they were going to preach, you may be sure that the whole population would turn out to listen. Sermons in those days in the country were very rarely delivered. As I have said, there were no pulpits in the churches then. A parson might hold a benefice for fifty years, and never once have written or composed a sermon. A preaching parson, one who regularly exhorted his people or expounded to them the Scriptures, would have been a wonder indeed, and thus the coming of the Friars and the revival of pulpit oratory was all the more welcome because the people had not become wearied by the too frequent iteration of truths which may be repeated so frequently as to lose their vital force. A sermon was an event in those days, and a preacher with any real gifts of oratory was looked upon as a prophet sent by God. Never was there a time when the people needed more to be taught the very rudiments of morality. Never had there been a time when people cared less whether their acts and words were right or wrong, true or false. It had almost come to this, that what a man thought would be to his profit, that was good; what would entail upon him a loss, that was evil.

And this brings me to another point, viz., the lawlessness and crime in country villages six hundred years ago. But before I can speak on that subject it is necessary that I should first try to give you some idea of the every-day life of your forefathers. What did they eat and drink? what did they wear? what did they do from day to day? Were they happy? content? prosperous? or was their lot a hard and bitter one? For according to the answer we get to questions such as these, so shall we be the better prepared to expect the people to have been peaceable citizens, or sullen, miserable, and dangerous ruffians, goaded to frequent outbursts of ferocious savagedom by hunger, oppression, hatred, and despair.

Six hundred years ago no parish in Norfolk had more than a part of its land under tillage. As a rule, the town or village, with its houses, great and small, consisted of a long street, the church and parsonage being situated about the middle of the parish. Not far off stood the manor house, with its hall where the manor courts were held, and its farm-buildings, dovecote, and usually its mill for grinding the corn of the tenants. No tenant of the manor might take his corn to be ground anywhere except at the lord's mill; and it is easy to see what a grievance this would be felt to be at times, and how the lord of the manor, if he were needy, unscrupulous, or extortionate, might grind the faces of the poor while he ground their corn. Behind most of the houses in the village might be seen a croft or paddock, an orchard or a small garden. But the contents of the gardens were very different from the vegetables we see now; there were, perhaps, a few cabbages, onions, parsnips, or carrots, and apparently some kind of beet or turnip. The potato had never been heard of.

As for the houses themselves, they were squalid enough for the most part. The manor house was often built of stone, when stone was to be had, or where, as in Norfolk, no stone was to be had, then of flint, as in so many of our church towers. Usually, however, the manor house was built in great part of timber. The poorer houses were dirty hovels, run up " anyhow," sometimes covered with turf, sometimes with thatch. None of them had chimneys. Six hundred years ago houses with chimneys were at least as rare as houses heated by hot-water pipes are now. Moreover, there were no brick houses. It is a curious fact that the art of making bricks seems to have been lost in England for some hundreds of years. The labourer's dwelling had no windows;

the hole in the roof which let out the smoke rendered windows unnecessary, and, even in the houses of the well-to-do, glass windows were rare. In many cases oiled linen cloth served to admit a feeble semblance of light, and to keep out the rain. The labourer's fire was in the middle of his house; he and his wife and children huddled round it, sometimes grovelling in the ashes; and going to bed meant flinging themselves down upon the straw which served them as mattress and feather bed, exactly as it does to the present day in the gipsy's tent in our byways. The labourer's only light by night was the smouldering fire. Why should he burn a rushlight when there was nothing to look at? and reading was an accomplishment which few labouring men were masters of.

As to the food of the majority, it was of the coarsest. The fathers of many a man and woman in every village in Norfolk can remember the time when the labourer looked upon wheat-bread as a rare delicacy; and those legacies which were left by kindly people a century or two ago, providing for the weekly distribution of so many *white* loaves to the poor, tell us of a time when the poor man's loaf was as dark as mud, and as tough as his shoe-leather. In the winter-time things went very hard indeed with all classes. There was no lack of fuel, for the

D

brakes and waste afforded turf which all might cut, and kindling which all had a right to carry away; but the poor horses and sheep and cattle were half starved for at least four months in the year, and one and all were much smaller than they are now. I doubt whether people ever fatted their hogs as we do. When the corn was reaped, the swine were turned into the stubble and roamed about the under-wood; and when they had increased their weight by the feast of roots and mast and acorns, they were slaughtered and salted for the winter fare, only so many being kept alive as might not prove burden-some to the scanty resources of the people. Salting down the animals for the winter consumption was a very serious expense. All the salt used was pro-duced by evaporation in *pans* near the seaside, and a couple of bushels of salt often cost as much as a sheep. This must have compelled the people to spare the salt as much as possible, and it must have been only too common to find the bacon more than rancid, and the ham alive again with maggots. If the salt was dear and scarce, sugar was unknown except to the very rich. The poor man had little to sweeten his lot. The bees gave him honey; and long after the time I am dealing with people left not only their hives to their children by will, but actually bequeathed a summer flight of bees to their friends;

while the hive was claimed by one, the next swarm might become the property of another.

As for the drink, it was almost exclusively water, beer, and cider.[1] Any one who pleased might brew beer without tax or license, and everybody who was at all before the world did brew his own beer according to his own taste. But in those days the beer was very different stuff from that which you are familiar with. To begin with, people did not use hops. Hops were not put into beer till long after the time we are concerned with. I dare say they flavoured their beer with horehound and other herbs, but they did not understand those tricks which brewers are said to practise now-a-days for making the beer "heady" and sticky and poisonous. I am not prepared to say the beer was better, or that you would have liked it; but I am pretty sure that in those days it was easier to get pure beer in a country village than it is now, and if a man chose to drink bad beer he had only himself to thank for it. There was no such monopoly as there is now. I am inclined to think that there were a very great many more people who sold beer in the country parishes than sell it now, and I am sorry to say that the beer-

---

[1] On a court roll of the manor of Whissonsete, of the date July 22, 1355, I find William Wate fined "iiij botell cideri quia fecit dampnum in bladis domini."

sellers in those days had the reputation of being rather a bad lot.[1] It is quite certain that they were very often in trouble, and of all the offences punished by fine at the manor courts none is more common than that of selling beer in false measures.

The method of cheating their customers by the beer-sellers was, we are told, exactly the contrary plan followed by our modern publicans. Now, when a man gets into a warm corner at the pot-house, they tell me that John Barleycorn is apt to serve out more drink than is good for him; but six hundred years ago the beer-seller made his profit, or tried to make it, by giving his customer less than he asked for. Tobacco was quite unknown; it was first brought into England about three hundred years after the

---

[1] The presentments of the beer-sellers seem to point to the existence of something like a licensing system among the lords of manors. I know not how otherwise to explain the frequency of the fines laid upon the whole class. Thus in a court-leet of the manor of Hockham, held the 20th of October, 1377, no less than fourteen women were fined in the aggregate 30s. 8d., who being *brassatores vendidere servisiam* (sic) *contra assisam*, one of these brewsters was fined as much as four shillings.

The earliest attempt to introduce uniformity in the measures of ale, &c., is the assize of Richard I., bearing date the 20th of November, 1197. It is to be found in " Walter of Coventry," vol. ii. p. 114 (Rolls Series). On the importance of this document see Stubbs' " Const. Hist.," vol. i. pp. 509, 573. On the *tasters* of bread and ale cf. " Dep. Keeper's 43rd Report,' p. 207.

days we are dealing with. When a man once sat himself down with his pot he had nothing to do but drink. He had no pipe to take off his attention from his liquor. If such a portentous sight could have been seen in those days as that of a man vomiting forth clouds of smoke from his mouth and nostrils, the beholders would have undoubtedly taken to their heels and run for their lives, protesting that the devil himself had appeared to them, breathing forth fire and flames. Tea and coffee, too, were absolutely unknown, unheard of; and wine was the rich man's beverage, as it is now. The fire-waters of our own time—the gin and the rum, which have wrought us all such incalculable mischief—were not discovered then. Some little ardent spirits, known under the name of *cordials*, were to be found in the better appointed establishments, and were kept by the lady of the house among her simples, and on special occasions dealt out in thimblefuls; but the vile grog, that maddens people now, our forefathers of six hundred years ago had never even tasted.

The absence of vegetable food for the greater part of the year, the personal dirt of the people, the sleeping at night in the clothes worn in the day, and other causes, made skin diseases frightfully common. At the outskirts of every town in England of any size there were crawling about emaciated creatures covered with loathsome sores, living heaven knows how. They were called by the common name of lepers, and probably the leprosy strictly so called was awfully common. But the children must have swarmed with vermin; and the itch, and the scurvy, and the ringworm, with other hideous eruptions, must have played fearful havoc with the weak and sickly.

As for the dress of the working classes, it was hardly dress at all. I doubt whether the great mass of the labourers in Norfolk had more than a single garment—a kind of tunic leaving the arms and legs bare, with a girdle of rope or leather round the waist, in which a man's knife was stuck, to use sometimes for hacking his bread, sometimes for stabbing an enemy in a quarrel. As for any cotton goods, such as are familiar to you all, they had never been dreamt of, and I suspect that no more people in Norfolk wore linen habitually than now wear silk.

Money was almost inconceivably scarce. The labourer's wages were paid partly in rations of food, partly in other allowances, and only partly in money; he had to take what he could get. Even the quit-rent, or what I have called the ground rent, was frequently compounded for by the tenant being required to find a pair of gloves, or a pound of cummin, or some other acknowledgment in lieu of a money payment; and one instance occurs among the Rougham charters of a man buying as much as 11½ acres, and paying for them partly in money and partly in barley.[1] Nothing shows more plainly the scarcity of money than the enormous interest that was paid for a loan. The only bankers were the Jews;[2] and when a man was once in their hands he was never likely to get out of their clutches again. But six hundred years ago the Jews had almost come to the end of their tether; and in the year 1290 they were driven out of the country, men, women, and children, with unutterable barbarity, only to be replaced by other bloodsuckers who were not a whit

---

[1] In the year 1276 halfpence and farthings were coined for the first time. This must have been a great boon to the poorer classes, and it evidently was felt to be a matter of great importance, insomuch that it was said to be the fulfilment of an ancient prophecy by the great seer Merlin, who had once foretold in mysterious language, that "there shall be half of the round." In the next century it appears that the want of small change had again made itself felt: for in the 2nd Richard II. we find the Commons setting forth in a petition to the King, that ". . . les ditz cōēs *n'on petit monoye pur paier pur les petites* mesures a grant damage des dites cōēs," and they beg "Le plese a dit S^r. le Roi et a son sage conseil de faire ordeiner Mayles et farthinges pur paier pur les petites mesures . . . et en eovre de charitée. . . ."—Rolls of Parl., vol. iii. p. 65.

[2] I am speaking of Norfolk and Suffolk, where the Jews, as far as I have seen, had it all their own way.

less mercenary, perhaps, but only less pushing and successful in their usury.

It is often said that the monasteries were the great supporters of the poor, and fed them in times of scarcity. It may be so, but I should like to see the evidence for the statement. At present I doubt the fact, at any rate as far as Norfolk goes.[1] On the contrary, I am strongly impressed with the belief that six hundred years ago the poor had no friends. The parsons were needy themselves. In too many cases one clergyman held two or three livings, took his tithes and spent them in the town, and left a chaplain with a bare subsistence to fill his place in the country. There was no parson's wife to drop in and speak a kind word—no clergyman's daughter to give a friendly nod, or teach the little ones at Sunday school—no softening influences, no sympathy, no kindliness. What could you expect of people with such dreary surroundings?—what but that which we know actually was the condition of affairs? The records of crime and outrage in Norfolk six

---

[1] The returns of the number of poor people supported by the monasteries, which are to be found in the "Valor Ecclesiasticus," are somewhat startling. Certainly the monasteries did not return *less* than they expended in alms. Note, too, the complaint of the St. Alban's men to Wat Tyler, who are said to have slandered the abbey "de retentione stipendiorum pauperum." Walsingham, i. 469.

hundred years ago are still preserved, and may be read by any one who knows how to decipher them. I had intended to examine carefully the entries of crime for this neighbourhood for the year 1286, and to give you the result this evening, but I have not had an opportunity of doing so. The work has been done for the hundred of North Erpingham by my friend Mr. Rye, and what is true for one part of Norfolk during any single year is not likely to be very different from what was going on in another.

The picture we get of the utter lawlessness of the whole county, however, at the beginning of King Edward's reign is quite dreadful enough. Nobody seems to have resorted to the law to maintain a right or redress a wrong, till every other method had been tried. Starting with the squires, if I may use the term, and those well-to-do people who ought to have been among the most law-abiding members of the community—we find them setting an example of violence and rapacity, bad to read of. One of the most common causes of offence was when the lord of the manor attempted to invade the rights of the tenants of the manor by setting up a fold on the heath, or *Bruary* as it was called. What the lord was inclined to do, that the tenants would try to do also, as when in 1272 John de Swanton set up a fold in the common fields at Billingford; whereupon the

D 2

other tenants pulled it down, and there was a serious disturbance, and the matter dragged on in the law courts for four years and more. Or as when the Prior of Wymondham impleads William de Calthorp for interfering with his foldage at Burnham; Calthorp replying that the Prior had no right to foldage, and that he (Calthorp) had the right to pull the fold down. In these cases, of course, there would be a general gathering and a riot, for every one's interest was at stake; but it was not only when some general grievance was felt that people in those days were ready for a row.

It really looks as if nothing was more easy than to collect a band of people who could be let loose anywhere to work any mischief. One man had a claim upon another for a debt, or a piece of land, or a right which was denied—had the claim, or fancied he had—and he seems to have had no difficulty in getting together a score or two of roughs to back him in taking the law into his own hands. As when John de la Wade in 1270 persuaded a band of men to help him in invading the manor of Hamon de Clere, in this very parish of Tittleshall, seizing the corn and threshing it, and, more wonderful still, cutting down timber, and *carrying it off*. There are actually two other cases of a precisely similar kind recorded this same year, one where a gang of fellows in broad day seems to have looted the manors of Dunton and Mileham; the other case was where a mob, under the leadership of three men, who are named, entered by force into the manor of Dunham, laid hands on a quantity of timber fit for building purposes, and took it away bodily! A much more serious case, however, occurred some years after this when two gentlemen of position in Norfolk, with twenty-five followers, who appear to have been their regular retainers, and a great multitude on foot and horse, came to Little Barningham, where in the Hall there lived an old lady, Petronilla de Gros; they set fire to the house in five places, dragged out the old lady, treated her with the most brutal violence, and so worked upon her fears that they compelled her to tell them where her money and jewels were, and, having seized them, I conclude that they left her to warm herself at the smouldering ruins of her mansion.

On another occasion there was a fierce riot at Rainham. There the manor had become divided into three portions, as we have seen was the case at Rougham. One Thomas de Hauville had one portion, and Thomas de Ingoldesthorp and Robert de Scales held the other two portions. Thomas de Hauville, peradventure, felt aggrieved because some rogue had not been whipped or tortured cruelly

enough to suit his notions of salutary justice, whereupon he went to the expense of erecting a brand new
pillory, and apparently a gallows too, to strike terror
into the minds of the disorderly. The other parceners of the manor were indignant at the act, and
collecting nearly sixty of the people of Rainham,
they pulled down the new pillory and utterly
destroyed the same. When the case came before
the judges, the defendants pleaded in effect that if
Thomas de Hauville had put up his pillory on his
own domain they would have had no objection, but
that he had invaded their rights in setting up his
gallows without their permission.

If the gentry, and they who ought to have known
better, set such an example, and gave their sanction
to outrage and savagery, it was only natural that the
lower orders should be quick to take their pattern by
their superiors, and should be only too ready to break
and defy the law. And so it is clear enough that
they were. In a single year, the year 1285, in the
hundred of North Erpingham, containing thirty-two
parishes, the catalogue of crime is so ghastly as
positively to stagger one. Without taking any
account of what in those days must have been looked
upon as quite minor offences—such as simple theft,
sheep-stealing, fraud, extortion, or harbouring felons
—there were eleven men and five women put upon

their trial for burglary, eight men and four women were murdered; there were five fatal fights, three men and two women being killed in the frays; and, saddest of all, there were five cases of suicide, among them two women, one of whom hanged herself, the other cut her throat with a razor. We have in the roll recording these horrors very minute particulars of the several cases, and we know too that, not many months before the roll was drawn up, at least eleven desperate wretches had been hanged for various offences, and one had been torn to pieces by horses for the crime of debasing the king's coin. It is impossible for us to realize the hideous ferocity of such a state of society as this; the women were as bad as the men, furious beldames, dangerous as wild beasts, without pity, without shame, without remorse; and finding life so cheerless, so hopeless, so very very dark and miserable, that when there was nothing to be gained by killing any one else they killed themselves.

Anywhere, anywhere out of the world !

Sentimental people who plaintively sigh for the good old times will do well to ponder upon these facts. Think, twelve poor creatures butchered in cold blood in a single year within a circuit of ten miles from your own door! Two of these unhappy victims were a couple of lonely women, apparently living together in their poverty, gashed and battered in the dead of the night, and left in their blood, stripped of their little all. The motive, too, for all this horrible housebreaking and bloodshed, being a lump of cheese or a side of bacon, and the shuddering creatures cowering in the corner of a hovel, being too paralyzed with terror to utter a cry, and never dreaming of making resistance to the wild-eyed assassins, who came to slay rather than to steal.

Let us turn from these scenes, which are too painful to dwell on; and, before I close, let me try and point to some bright spots in the village life of six hundred years ago. If the hovels of the labourer were squalid, and dirty, and dark, yet there was not —no, there was not—as much difference between them and the dwelling of the former class, the employers of labour. Every man who had any house at all had some direct interest in the land; he always had some rood or two that he could call his own; his allotment was not large, but then there were no large farmers. I cannot make out that there was any one in Rougham who farmed as much as two hundred acres all told. What we now understand by tenant farmers were a class that had not yet come into existence. Where a landlord was non-resident he farmed his estate by a bailiff, and if any one wanted to give up an occupation for a time he let it with all that it contained. Thus, when Alice the divorced made up her mind in 1318 to go away from Rougham —perhaps on a pilgrimage—perhaps to Rome—who knows?—she let her house and land, and all that was upon it, live and dead stock, to her sister Juliana for three years. The inventory included not only the sheep and cattle, but the very hoes and pitchforks, and sacks; and everything, to the minutest particular, was to be returned without damage at the end of the term, or replaced by an equivalent. But this lady, a lady of birth and some position, certainly did not have two hundred acres under her hands, and would have been a very small personage indeed, side by side with a dozen of our West Norfolk farmers to-day. The difference between the labourer and the farmer was, I think, less six hundred years ago than it is now. Men climbed up the ladder by steps that were more gently graduated; there was no great gulf fixed between the employer and the employed.

I can tell you nothing of the amusements of the people in those days. I doubt whether they had any more amusement than the swine or the cows had. Looking after the fowls or the geese, hunting for the hen's nest in the furze brake, and digging out a fox or a badger, gave them an hour's excitement or interest now and again. Now and then a wandering minstrel came by, playing upon his rude instrument,

and now and then somebody would come out from
Lynn, or Yarmouth, or Norwich, with some new
batch of songs for the most part scurrilous and
coarse, and listened to much less for the sake of the
music than for the words. Nor were books so rare
as has been asserted. There were even story-books
in some houses, as where John Senekworth, bailiff
for Merton College, at Gamlingay in Cambridgeshire,
possessed, when he died in 1314, three books of
romance ; but then he was a thriving yeoman with
carpets in his house, or hangings for the walls.[1]

There was a great deal more coming and going in
the country villages than there is now, a great deal
more to talk about, a great deal more doing. The
courts of the manor were held periodically, and the
free tenants were bound to attend and carry on a
large amount of petty business. Then there were
the periodical visitations by the Archdeacon and
the Rural Dean, and now and then more august
personages might be seen with a host of mounted
followers riding along the roads. The Bishop of
Norwich was always on the move when he was in
his diocese ; his most favourite places of residence
were North Elmham and Gaywood ; at both of these
places he had a palace and a park ; that meant that
there were deer there and hunting, and all the good

[1] Rogers' "Hist. of Prices," vol. i. p. 124.

and evil that seems to be inseparable from haunches of vension. Nay, at intervals, even the Archbishop of Canterbury himself, the second man in the kingdom, came down to hold a visitation in Norfolk, and, exactly 602 years ago the great Archbishop Peckham spent some time in the county, and though I do not think he came near Rougham or Tittleshall, I think it not improbable that his coming may have had some influence in bringing about the separation between Peter Romayn and Matilda de Cringleford, and the divorce of poor Alice from John of Thyrsford.

That year, 1280, or just 602 years ago, when Archbishop Peckham paid his visit to Norfolk, was a very disastrous year for the farmers. It was the beginning of a succession of bad seasons and floods even worse than any that we have known. The rain began on the 1st of August, and we are told that it continued to fall for twenty-four hours, and then came a mighty wind such as men had never known the like of; the waters were out, and there was a great flood, and houses and windmills and bridges were swept away. Nay, we hear of a sad loss of life, and many poor people were drowned, and many lost their all; flocks, and herds, and corn and hay being whelmed in the deluge. In November there was a frightful tempest, the lightning doing extensive damage; and just at Christmas-time the frost set in with such severity as no man had known before. The river Thames was frozen over above London Bridge, so that men crossed it with horses and carts, and when the frost broke up on the 2nd of February there was such an enormous accumulation of ice and snow that five of the arches of London Bridge blew up, and all over the country the same destruction of bridges was heard of.

Next year and the year after that, things went very badly with your forefathers, and one of the saddest stories that we get from a Norfolk chronicler who was alive at the time is one in which he tells us that, owing to the continuous rain during these three years, there was an utter failure in garden produce, as well as of the people's hope of harvest. The bad seasons seem to have gone on for six or seven years; but by far the worst calamity which Norfolk ever knew was the awful flood of 1287, when by an incursion of the sea a large district was laid under water, and hundreds of unfortunate creatures were drowned in the dead of the night, without warning. Here, on the higher level, people were comparatively out of harm's way, but it is impossible to imagine the distress and agony that there must have been in other parts of the county not twenty miles from where we are this evening.

After that dreadful year I think there was a change for the better, but it must have been a long time before the county recovered from the "agricultural distress;" and I strongly suspect that the cruel and wicked persecution of the Jews, and the cancelling of all debts due to them by the landlords and the farmers, was in some measure owing to the general bankruptcy which the succession of bad seasons had brought about. Men found themselves hopelessly insolvent, and there was no other way of cancelling their obligations than by getting rid of their creditors. So when the king announced that all the Jews should be transported out of the realm, you may be sure that there were very few Christians who were sorry for them. There had been a time when the children of Israel had spoiled the Egyptians—was it not fitting that another time should have come when the children of Israel should themselves be spoiled?

The year of the great flood was the frequent talk, of course, of all your forefathers who overlived it, and here in this neighbourhood it must have acquired an additional interest from the fact that Bishop Middleton died the year after it, and his brothers then parted with their Rougham property.

Nor was this all, for Bishop Middleton's successor in the see of Norwich came from this immediate neighbourhood also. This was Ralph Walpole, son

of the lord of the manor of Houghton, in which parish
the bishop himself had inherited a few acres of land.
In less than forty years no less than three bishops
had been born within five miles of where we are this
evening: Roger de Wesenham,[1] who became Bishop
of Lichfield in 1245; William Middleton, who had
just died; and Ralph Walpole, who succeeded him.
There must have been much stir in these parts when
the news was known. The old people would tell
how they had seen "young master Ralph" many a
time when he was a boy scampering over Massingham Heath, or coming to pay his respects to the
Archdeacon at the Lyng House, or talking of foreign
parts with old James de Ferentino or Peter Romayn.
Now he had grown to be a very big man indeed, and
there were many eyes watching him on both sides
of the water. He had a very difficult game to play
during the eleven years he was Bishop of Norwich,
for the king was dreadfully in need of money, and,
being desperate, he resorted to outrageous methods
of squeezing it from those whom he could frighten
and force, and the time came at last when the bishops
and the clergy had to put a bold face on and to resist
the tyranny and lawless rapacity of the sovereign.

---

[1] The names of several members of the bishop's family occur
in the Rougham Charters as attesting witnesses, and a Roger
de Wesenham is found among them more than once.

And this reminds me that though archdeacons, and bishops, and even an archbishop, in those days might be and were very important and very powerful personages, they were all very small and insignificant in comparison with the great King Edward, the king who at this time was looked upon as one of the most mighty and magnificent kings in all the world. He, too, paid many a visit to Norfolk six hundred years ago. He kept his Christmas at Burgh in 1280, and in 1284 he came down with the good Queen Eleanor and spent the whole of Lent in the county; and next year, again, they were in your immediate neighbourhood, making a pilgrimage to Walsingham. A few years after this he seems to have spent a week or two within five miles of where we are; he came to Castle Acre, and there he stayed at the great priory whose ruins you all know well. There a very stirring interview took place between the king and Bishop Walpole, and a number of other bishops, and great persons who had come down as a deputation to expostulate with the king, and respectfully to protest against the way in which he was robbing his subjects, and especially the clergy, whom he had been for years plundering in the most outrageous manner. The king gave the deputation no smooth words to carry away, but he sent them off with threatening frowns and insults and in hot anger. Some days after this he was at Massingham, and one of his letters has been preserved, dated from Massingham, 30th of January, 1296, so that it is almost certain the great king passed one night there at least. It is a little difficult to understand what the king was doing at Massingham, for there was no great man living there, and no great mansion. Sometimes I have thought that the king rode out from Castle Acre to see what state the Walpoles of those times were keeping up at Houghton. Had not that audacious Bishop Walpole dared to speak plainly to his Grace the week before? But the more probable explanation is that the king went to Massingham to visit a small religious house or monastery which had been recently founded there. I suspect it had already got into debt and was in difficulties, and it is possible that the king's visit was made in the interest of the foundation. At any rate, there the king stayed; but though he was in Norfolk more than once after this, he never was so near you again, and that visit was one which your forefathers were sure to talk about to the end of their lives.

. . . . . .

And these were the days of old. But now that we have looked back upon them as they appear through the mists of centuries, the distance distorting some things, obscuring others, but leaving upon us, on the whole, an impression that, after all, these men and women of the past, whose circumstances were so different from our own, were perhaps not so very unlike what we should be if our surroundings were as theirs. Now that we have come to that conclusion, if indeed we have come to it, let me ask you all a question or two. Should we like to change with those forefathers of ours, whose lives were passed in this parish in the way I have attempted to describe, six hundred years ago? Were the former times better than these? Has the world grown worse as it has grown older? Has there been no progress, but only decline?

My friends, the people who lived in this village six hundred years ago were living a life hugely below the level of yours. They were more wretched in their poverty, they were incomparably less prosperous in their prosperity, they were worse clad, worse fed, worse housed, worse taught, worse tended, worse governed; they were sufferers from loathsome diseases which you knew nothing of; the very beasts of the field were dwarfed and stunted in their growth, and I do not believe there were any giants in the earth in those days. The death-rate among the children must have been tremendous. The disregard of human life was so callous that we can hardly conceive it. There was everything to harden, nothing to soften; everywhere oppression, greed, and fierce-ness. Judged by our modern standards, the people of our county village were beyond all doubt coarser, more brutal, and more wicked, than they are. Pro-gress is slow, but there has been progress. The days that are, are not what they should be; we still want reforms, we need much reforming ourselves; but the former days were not better than these, whatever these may be; and if the next six hundred years exhibit as decided an advance as the last six centuries have brought about, and if your children's children of the coming time rise as much above your level in sentiment, material comfort, knowledge, intelligence, and refinement, as you have risen above the level which your ancestors attained to, though even then they will not cease to desire better things, they will nevertheless have cause for thankfulness such as you may well feel to-night as you look back upon what you have escaped from, and reflect upon what you are.

III.

DAILY LIFE IN A MEDIÆVAL MONASTERY.

" Now I think on't,
They should be good men ; their affairs as righteous :
But all hoods make not monks."

[THE commemoration of the birth of Martin Luther, which people would have called his quater-centenary if they had not been deterred by the terrific appearance of so huge a word, was the occasion of many preachments and much lecturing, besides a great deal of heroic talk in public and private. With so much to encourage cynicism and persiflage among us it was comforting to find that the instinct of hero-worship is not quite dead, and that the story of a great man's life still stirs the heart. It was inevitable that, among the many utterances with which we were treated in the year 1883, many should be very foolish, and not a few mischievous and erroneous. Itinerant Windbags are rarely scrupulous about their

9   113

facts, and the allusive style flavoured with stinging invective is far more telling than any historical narrative, however picturesque and eloquent it may be. Luther the Monk will always be a more attractive subject in the lecture hall than Luther the Theologian, and an audience prepared to be harrowed and shocked will greedily listen to broad hints about *abominations*—the word is a very favourite one—which the author could disclose, but mercifully withholds in pity for the shuddering hearts of a too sensitive assembly. The consequence was that an altogether disproportionate amount of declamation was wasted up and down the country by gentlemen on the stump, in girding at monks and nuns, their vices and crimes, till some men's minds were not a little exercised, and some, horrified by what they were told, asked in their perplexity, " Can these things be? " The present writer knows nothing of the condition of the German Religious Houses in the fifteenth or the sixteenth century, and not as much as he would wish to learn of the condition of the English houses during the same period, but he has been painfully convinced that the peripatetic orators are about as qualified to lecture upon the subject as he is to lecture on astronomy.

It was while musing in my solitude upon the harm

done by ignorant pretenders in sowing error broadcast in the waste places of the world that I received a call from one of the class, who came to beg my countenance for a lecture upon Luther the Monk and Monkery. He was a vociferous personage and prodigal of his words. He added to all his sins this one, that he did not know when to go. He had no tact, only talk. Irritated at last beyond endurance, my normal suavity forsook me, and I spoke with brutal plainness. Of course he was wroth, and pressed for an explanation. In a weak moment I yielded. "To begin with," said I, "Luther, strictly speaking, was not a monk at all!"[1] It was a foolish speech : first, because it made my friend an offender for a word ; and, secondly, because there was more truth in it than the man was capable of understanding or was prepared to receive ; but it had the effect of ridding me of a bore. As he took his leave he shot at me this Parthian shaft—"If you are above learning, sir," he said, "perhaps teaching might not be beneath you. Could you not, for instance, let the world know something about monks and monasteries some day ? Even I, ignorant as you pronounce me, have heard of your lecturing on a thirteenth-century village. Why not try a thirteenth-century monastery

[1] He belonged to the order of Friars Eremite under the Augustinian Rule.

next ?" I politely thanked him for his valuable suggestion, and promised to give it my respectful attention. The following sketch is the outcome of our interview. "Facit indignatio versus."]

.   .   .   .   .   .

It may be assumed as a fact which scarcely requires to be more than stated that there are few subjects which the great mass of Englishmen are so curiously ignorant of as the History of Monasticism, of the constitution of the various Orders, of the fortunes of any single religious house, or the discipline to which its members were, in theory at least, compelled to submit. The assumption being granted, it may naturally be asked, How is such ignorance to be accounted for ? It is due to more causes than one, but chiefly and primarily to the vastness of the subject itself.

When the monasteries were suppressed by Henry VIII. there was an utter obliteration of an order of things which had existed in our island for certainly more than a thousand years, and how much longer it is impossible to say. The names of religious houses which are known to have existed before the Norman Conquest count by hundreds ; the names of men and women who presided over such houses during the centuries preceding that event count by thousands. Some of these religious houses had passed through the strangest vicissitudes; they had been pillaged again and again; they had been burnt by Danish marauders; their inmates driven out into the wilderness or ruthlessly put to the sword; their lands given over to the spoiler or gone out of cultivation; their very existence in some cases almost forgotten; yet they had revived again and again from their ashes. When William the Conqueror came among us, and that stern rule of his began, there was scarcely a county in England and Wales in which one or more religious houses were not to be found, and during his reign of twenty-one years about thirty new monasteries of one sort or another were added to those already existing.

To begin with, the very word monastery is a misnomer: the word is a Greek word, and means the dwelling-place of a solitary person, living in seclusion. But, misnomer though it be, the employment of the word in a sense so widely different from that which it first bore, until it got to designate the dwelling-place of a corporate body, among whom no solitude was allowed and privacy was almost impossible, is of itself very significant as indicating the stages through which the original idea of monasticism passed.

It was natural enough, when society was in a condition of profound disorganization, and sensuality and violence were in the ascendant, that men and women of gentle nature should become convinced that the higher life could only be lived in lonely retirement, far from the sound of human voices and the contact of human creatures, whose very nearness almost implies sin. But what a vast step from this to that other conviction which the developed form of monasticism expresses, when experience has convinced the devout searcher after God that no great work can be done in improving the world, or raising the tone of society, or in battling with our own weaknesses and vices, except by earnest, resolute, and disciplined co-operation. It is when we draw together that we are strong, and strongest when we are labouring shoulder to shoulder for some common object, and that no mean and sordid one; it is then that we best find deliverance from our self-deception and most inveterate delusions, whilst living in the light of other's eyes, and subjected to the influence and control of a healthy and well-instructed public opinion.

In the thirteenth century (and I shall as much as possible confine myself to the limits of that period), a monastery meant what we now understand it to mean—viz., the abode of a society of men or women who lived together in common—who were supposed to partake of common meals; to sleep together in one common dormitory; to attend certain services together in their common church; to transact certain business or pursue certain employments in the sight and hearing of each other in the common cloister; and, when the end came, to be laid side by side in the common graveyard, where in theory none but members of the order could find a resting-place for their bones. When I say "societies of men and women" I am again reminded that the other term, "convent," has somehow got to be used commonly in a mistaken sense. People use the word as if it signified a religious house tenanted exclusively by women. The truth is that a convent is nothing more than a Latin name for an association of *persons* who have *come together* with a view to live for a common object and to submit to certain rules in the ordering of their daily lives. The monastery was the common dwelling-place: the convent was the society of persons inhabiting it; and the ordinary formula used when a body of monks or nuns execute any corporate act—such as buying or selling land— by any legal instrument is, "The Prior and Convent of the Monastery of the Holy Trinity at Norwich;" "the Abbot and Convent of the Monastery of St. Peter's, Westminster;" "the Abbess and Convent of the Monastery of St. Mary and St. Bernard at Lacock," and so on.

Bearing in mind, then, that the term convent has to do with a corporation of men or women united into an organized society, and that the term monastery can strictly be applied only to the buildings—the *domus*, in which that society has its home—it will be well at starting that we should endeavour to gain some notion of the general plan of these buildings first, and when we have done that that we should proceed to deal next with the constitution of the society itself and the daily routine of conventual life.

A monastery in theory then was, as it was called, a Religious House. It was supposed to be the home of people whose lives were passed in the worship of God, and in taking care of their own souls, and making themselves fit for a better world than this hereafter. As for this world, it was lying in wickedness; if men remained in this wicked world they would most certainly become contaminated by all its pollutions; the only chance of ever attaining to holiness lay in a man or woman's turning his back upon the world and running away from it. It was no part of a monk's duty to reform the world; all he had to do was to look after himself, and to save himself from the wrath to come. It is hardly overstating the case if I say that a monastery was not intended to be a benevolent institution; and if a great religious house became, as it almost inevitably did become, the centre of civilization and refinement, from which radiated light and warmth and incalculable blessings far and wide, these results flowed naturally from that growth and development which the original founders had never looked forward to or could have foreseen, but it was never contemplated as an end to be aimed at in the beginning. Being a home for religious men, whose main business was to spend their days and nights in worshipping God, the first requisite, the first and foremost, the *sine qua non* was, that there should be a church.

On the church of a monastery, as a rule, no amount of money spent, no amount of lavish ornament or splendour of decoration, was grudged. Sculpture and painting, jewels and gold, gorgeous hangings, and stained-glass that the moderns vainly attempt to imitate, the purple and fine linen of the priestly vestments, embroidery that to this hour remains unapproachable in its delicacy of finish and in the perfect harmony of colours—all these were to be found in almost incredible profusion in our monastic churches. You hear some people work themselves into a frenzy against the idolatrous worship of our forefathers ; but to a monk of a great monastery his church was his one idol—to possess a church that should surpass all others in magnifi-

E

cence, and which could boast of some special unique glory—that seemed to a monk something worth living for. The holy rood at Bromholm, the holy thorn at Glastonbury, were possessions that brought world-wide renown to the monasteries in which they were found, and gave a lustre to the churches in which they were deposited; and the intense *esprit de corps*, the passionate loyalty, of a monk to his monastery is a sentiment which we in our time find it so extremely difficult to understand that we can hardly bring ourselves to believe that it could exist without some subtle intermixture of crafty selfishness as its ruling force and motive.

The church of a monastery was the heart of the place. It was not that the church was built for the monastery, but the monastery existed for the church; there were hundreds and thousands of churches without monasteries, but there could be no monastery without a church. The monks were always at work on the church, always spending money upon it, always adding to it, always "restoring" it; it was always needing repair. We are in the habit of saying, "Those old monks knew how to build; look at their work—see how it stands!" But we are very much mistaken if we suppose that in the twelfth or the thirteenth or the fourteenth century there was no bad building. On the contrary, nothing is more common in the monastic annals than the notices of how this and that tower fell down, and how this and that choir was falling into ruins, and how this or that abbot got into debt by his mania for building. There was an everlasting tinkering going on at the church; and the surest token that a monastery was in a bad way was that its church was in a shabby condition.

The church was, almost invariably, built in the form of a cross, facing east and west, the long limb of the cross being called the nave, the cross limbs being called the transepts, and the shorter limb, or head of the cross, being called the choir. The choir, as a rule, was occupied exclusively by the monks or nuns of the monastery. The servants, workpeople, and casual visitors who came to worship were not admitted into the choir; *they* were supposed to be present only on sufferance. The church was built for the use of the monks; it was *their* private place of worship.

Almost as essential to the idea of a monastery as the church was the cloister or great quadrangle, inclosed on all sides by the high walls of the monastic buildings. Its usual position was on the south of the church, to gain as much of the sun's rays as possible, and to insure protection from the northerly and easterly winds in the bitter season. All round this quadrangle ran a covered arcade, whose roof, leaning against the high walls, was supported on the inner side by an open trellis work in stone—often exhibiting great beauty of design and workmanship—through which light and air was admitted into the arcade.[1] The open space not roofed in was called the *garth*, and was sometimes a plain grass plat and sometimes was planted with shrubs, a fountain of running water being often found in the centre, which afforded a pleasant object for the eye to rest on. The cloister was really the living-place of the monks. Here they pursued their daily avocations, here they taught their school, they transacted their business, they spent their time and pursued their studies, always in society, co-operating and consulting, and, as a rule, knowing no privacy.

" But surely a monk always lived in a cell, didn' he ? "

The sooner we get rid of that delusion the better.

Be it understood that until Henry II. founded the Carthusian Abbey of Witham, in 1178, there was

[1] In other words the thirteenth-century monk passed far the greater portion of his time in the open air, except that there was a roof over his head. As time went on, and monks became more self-indulgent, they did not by any means like the draught and exposure in the cloister, and the old-fashioned open arcade were glazed, and the old open walks were turned into splendid lounges, comfortable and luxurious, such as the cloisters of Gloucester could be made into at a small outlay at the present day.

no such thing known in England as a monk's *cell*, as we understand the term. It was a peculiarity of the Carthusian order, and when it was first introduced it was regarded as a startling novelty for any privacy or anything approaching solitude to be tolerated in a monastery. The Carthusian system never found much favour in England. The Carthusians never had more than nine houses, all told ; the discipline was too rigid, the rule too severe, the loneliness too dreadful for our tastes and for our climate. In the thirteenth century, if I mistake not, there were only two monasteries in England in which monks or nuns could boast of having any privacy, any little corner of their own to turn into, any place where they could enjoy the luxury of retirement, any private study such as every boy nowadays, in a school of any pretension, expects to have provided for himself, and without which we assume that nobody can read and write for an hour.

The cloister arcade was said to have four *walks*. The south walk ran along the south wall of the nave, the north walk was bounded by the refectory or great dining hall, the east walk extended along the south transept, and where the transept ended there usually came a narrow passage called a *slype*, passing between the end of the transept and the chapter-house, which may be described as the council-chamber of the

convent. Beyond the chapter-house, and abutting
partly upon the east wall of the cloister, but extending far beyond it till, in some cases, it made with
the refectory a block of buildings in the form of a T,
ran the dormitory or common sleeping-place for the
fraternity. The dormitory was always approached
by steps, for it was invariably constructed over a
range of vaulted chambers, which served for various
purposes ; one of these chambers was set apart for
the reception of those monks who had been subjected
to the monthly bleedings which all were supposed to
require, and which all were compelled to submit to,
that so by a mechanical process, if in no other way,
the flesh might be subdued. The beds of the monks
were arranged along the walls of the dormitory, at
regular intervals ; and in some monasteries a wains-
cot partition separated the sleepers from each other,
thus making for each a little cubicle, with a low door
leading into it. The broad passage, running from
end to end, between the sleeping-places in the dormitory was strewn with rushes ; and at the end
opposite to the flight of stairs were the latrines or
washing-places, which were open to the air, and
under which was always a sewer that could be
flushed by a water-course hard by.

In the dormitory and the latrines lights were kept
burning through the night ; a provision necessary,

if for no other reason, because the services in the
church at night-time had to be kept up and attended
by the whole house. They who went from the
dormitory to the church always passed under cover—
sometimes by going through the cloister, sometimes
by passing straight into the transept.

We have been round three sides of the cloister:
on the north the church; on the east the chapter-
house and dormitory; on the south the refectory.
There remain the buildings abutting on the west
wall. In the arrangement of these no strict rule was
observed. But generally the western buildings were
dedicated to the cellarer's hall with cellars under it,
the pitanciar's and kitchener's offices or *chequers* as
they were called, and a guest-chamber for the reception of distinguished strangers and for the duties of
hospitality, to which great importance was attached.

These were the main buildings, the essential
buildings of a monastery great or small. Where a
monastery was rich enough to indulge in luxuries of
" modern improvements and all the best appliances,"
there was hardly any limit to the architectural freaks
that might be indulged in. There were the in-
firmary and the hospital; the calefactory or warm-
ing apparatus, the recreation hall and the winter
hall, the locutorium and the common hall, and I
know not what besides. You observe I have as yet

said nothing about the library. I must remind you that in the thirteenth century the number of books in the world was, to say the least, small. A library of five hundred volumes would, in those days, have been considered an important collection, and, after making all due allowances for ridiculous exaggeration which have been made by ill-informed writers on the subject, it may safely be said that nobody in the thirteenth century—at any rate in England—would have erected a large and lofty building as a receptacle for books, simply because nobody could have contemplated the possibility of filling it. Here and there amongst the larger and more important monasteries there were undoubtedly collections of books, the custody of which was intrusted to an accredited officer; but the time had not yet come for making libraries well stored with such priceless treasures as Leland, the antiquary, saw at Glastonbury, just before that magnificent foundation was given as a prey to the spoilers. A library, in any such sense as we now understand the term, was not only no essential part of a monastery in those days, but it may be said to have been a rarity.

But if the thirteenth century monastery possessed necessarily no great Reading-Room, the Scriptorium, or Writing-Room, was almost an essential adjunct. In the absence of the printing-press, the demand for skilled writers and copyists throughout the country was enormous. In the Scriptorium all the business, now transacted by half a dozen agents and their clerks, was carried on. The land of the country in those days was subdivided to an extent that it is now almost impossible for us to realize, and the tenure under which the small patches of arable or meadow-land were held was sometimes very complex and intricate. The small patches were perpetually changing hands, being bought or sold, settled upon trustees, or let out for a term of years, and every transaction would be registered in the books of the monastery interested, while the number of conveyances, leases, and enfeofments made out in the course of the year was incalculable. In such an abbey as that of Bury St. Edmunds a small army of writers must have been constantly employed in the business department of the Scriptorium alone. Obviously it became a great writing-school, where the copyists consciously or unconsciously wrote according to the prevailing fashion of the place; and there have been, and there are, experts who could tell you whether this or that document was or was not written in this or that monastic Scriptorium. Paper was very little used, and the vellum and parchment required constituted a heavy item of expense. Add to this the production of school-books and all materials used for carrying on

E 2

the education work, the constant replacement of
church service books which the perpetual thumbing
and fingering would subject to immense wear and
tear, the great demand for music which, however
simple, required to be written out large and conspicuous in order to be read with ease, and you get
a rather serious list of the charges upon the sta-
tionery department of a great abbey.

But though by far the greater portion of work done
in the Scriptorium was mere office work, the educational department, if I may so term it, being
subsidiary, it must not be forgotten that the literary
and the historical department also was represented
in the Scriptorium of every great monastery. In the
thirteenth century men never kept diaries or journals
of their own daily lives, but monasteries did. In
theory, every religious house recorded its own annals,
or kept a chronicle of great events that were happen-
ing in Church and State. Where a monastery had
kept its chronicle going for a long time, it got to be
regarded almost as a sacred book, and was treated
with great veneration : it lay in a conspicuous place
in the Scriptorium, and was under the care of an
officer who alone was permitted to make entries in
it. When any great piece of news was brought to
the monastery that seemed worth putting on record,
the person giving the information wrote out his

version of the story on a loose piece of parchment, and slipped his communication into the book of annals for the authorized compiler to make use of in any way that seemed best to him, after due examination of evidence. This was the rule in all monastic houses. Unfortunately, however, as it is with the journals or diaries of men and women of the nineteenth century, so it was with the journals and diaries of monks of the thirteenth, they evidently were kept by fits and starts; and before the fourteenth century was half out, the practice of keeping up these diaries in all but the larger monasteries had come to an end.

Before passing on from the Library and Scriptorium, on which a great deal more might easily be said, it is necessary that one caution should be given; I know not how that notion originated or how it has taken such hold of the minds of ninety-nine men out of a hundred, that the monks as a class were students or scholars or men of learning; as far as the English monasteries of the thirteenth century are concerned, I am sure that the notion is altogether erroneous. If we except some few of the larger and nobler monasteries, which from first to last seem always to have been centres of culture, enlightenment, and progress, the monks were no more learned than the nuns. As a class, students, scholars, and

teachers they were not. When King John died, in
1216, a little learning went a long way, and whatever
the Norman Conquest did for England (and it did a
great deal), it certainly was not an event calculated
to increase the love of study, or likely to make men
bookish pundits.

I should only confuse my readers if I dwelt more
at length upon the buildings of a monastery. It is
enough for the present that we should understand
clearly that the essential buildings were (1) the
church, (2) the cloister, (3) the dormitory, (4) the
refectory, (5) the chapter-house. In these five
buildings the life of the convent was carried on.
Having said thus much we will pass on to the
corporation itself—that which strictly was called the
convent; and for convenience and distinctness it
will be as well if we use that word *convent* in the
more accurate sense and employ it only as signifying
the corporate body of persons occupying those
buildings of which I have been speaking, and which
in their aggregate were called a *monastery*.

Once more I think it necessary to start with a
caution. Not only do I propose to take no account
here of that large class of conventuals which comprehended the mendicant order or friars as they are
called, but I must needs pass by with little or no
notice the various orders of regular canons—*i.e.*

canons living under a rule. The friars came into England first in 1220. During the thirteenth century they were, so to speak, upon their trial; and from the first the monks and the friars were essentially opposed in the ideal of their daily lives. So with the very numerous houses of canons regular up and down the land. They and the monks did not love one another, and when I speak of monks and their houses it will be advisable to exclude from our consideration the friars on the one hand and the canons on the other, and, in fact, to limit ourselves to that view of conventual life which the great English monasteries under the rule of St. Benedict afford.

At the time of the Norman Conquest it may be said that all English monks were professedly under one and the same Rule—the famous Benedictine Rule. The Rule of a monastery was the constitution or code of laws, which regulated the discipline of the house, and the Rule of St. Benedict dates back as far as the sixth century, though it was not introduced into England for more than a hundred years after it had been adopted elsewhere. Four hundred years is a very long time for any constitution or code of law to last unchanged, and though the English monasteries professedly were living according to the Benedictine Rule during all the

Saxon and the Danish times, yet there is too much reason to believe that if St. Benedict could have risen from the dead in the days of Edward the Confessor and made a visitation of many an English house, he would have been rather astonished to be told that the monks were living according to his Rule.

About one hundred and fifty years before the Conquest, a great reformation had been attempted of the French monasteries, which it was said had fallen into a state of great decay as far as discipline and fervour were concerned, and a revision of the old rule had been found necessary, the reformers breaking away from the old Benedictines and subjecting themselves to a new and improved Rule. These first reformers were called *Cluniac* monks, from the great Abbey of Clugni, in Burgundy, in which the new order of things had begun. The first English house of reformed or Cluniac monks was founded at Lewes, in Sussex, eleven years after the Conquest, by Gundrada, a step-daughter of William the Conqueror, and her husband, William, Earl of Warrene and Surrey. The Cluniacs were at first famous for the simplicity of their lives and the strictness of their discipline, but as time went on they became too rich and so too luxurious, and at last they too needed reforming, and a new reformer arose. In this case the real moving spirit of reformation was an Englishman, one Stephen Harding, probably a Dorsetshire man, who was brought up at the Benedictine monastery of Sherborne, and in the course of events chosen Abbot of the monastery of Citeaux, where St. Bernard became his ardent disciple, and where the two enthusiasts, working cordially together, brought about that second reform of the Benedictines which resulted in the founding of the great Cistercian order.

Thus, without looking too minutely into the matter, we find that when the thirteenth century opens, or if you will, when Henry III. came to the throne in 1216, there were three great orders of monks in England—the old Benedictines, who had held houses and lands for centuries; the Cluniacs, who were the reformed Benedictines; and the Cistercians, who may be styled the reformed Cluniacs. But inasmuch as the architectural and other reforms among the Cistercians were many and peculiar, it will again be advisable to pass by these peculiarities without remark.

.   .   .   .   .   .

The constitution of every convent, great or small, was monarchical. The head of the house was almost an absolute sovereign, and was called the Abbot. His dominions often extended, even in

England, over a very wide tract of country, and sometimes over several minor monasteries which were called Cells. Thus the Abbot of St. Alban's had under himself the cell of Tynemouth in Northumberland and two others in Norfolk—viz., Binham and Wymondham, the latter of which eventually became an independent abbey—and the heads of these cells or subject houses were called Priors. An *abbey* was a monastery which was independent. A priory was a monastery which in theory or in fact was subject to an abbey. All the Cluniac monasteries in England were thus said to be alien priories, because they were mere cells of the great Abbey of Clugni in France, to which each priory paid heavy tribute; while the priors were almost always foreigners, and always appointed by the Abbot of Clugni, and responsible to him much in the same way as a Pacha is to his suzerain the Sultan. On the other hand, the Cistercian houses were all abbeys, and their abbots sovereigns in alliance or confederation with one another, and exercising over their several convents supreme jurisdiction, though recognizing the Abbot of Citeaux as their over-lord. The abbot not only had a separate residence within the monastery and lived apart from his monks, but he had his separate estate for the maintenance of his dignity, and to bear the very heavy expenses which that dignity necessitated, and he had the patronage of every office in the convent. These officers were numerous. The first of them was the prior, who was the abbot's prime minister and head of the executive and the abbot's representative in his absence. Under him was the sub-prior, sometimes a third prior, and then a number of functionaries, to whom, as in the case of the abbot, separate estates were assigned out of which they were bound to provide for certain charges which they were called upon to meet as best they could, while a complicated system of finance provided for the surplus of one office being applied when necessary for the deficiency of another.

In the great Abbey of Evesham a very elaborate constitution was drawn up and agreed to in the year 1214, after a long dispute between the abbot and convent which had lasted for several years, and this scheme has come down to us.

From it we find that certain officers (obedientiaries was their technical name) were charged with providing certain articles out of the revenue of the office. The prior, to whom no mean share of the revenues was assigned, had to provide the parchment that might be required for business purposes or for legal instruments and all other materials for the scriptorium, except ink. The manciple was to provide all wine and mead, the keeping up the stock of earthenware cups, jugs, basins, and other vessels, together with the lamps and oil. The precentor had to find all the ink used, and all colour required for illumination, the materials for book-binding, and the keeping the organ in repair. To the chamberlain were assigned certain revenues for providing all the clothing of the monks, it being stipulated that the abbot's dress was not to be paid for out of the fund. In the same way certain small tithes are apportioned for buying basins, jugs, and towels for the guests' chamber; while all rents levied from the various tenants paid not in money, but in kind—as, *e.g.*, capons, eggs, salmon, eels, herrings, &c.—were to be passed to the account of the kitchener. Every monk bearing office was bound to present his accounts for audit at regular intervals, and the rolls on which these accounts were inscribed exist in very large numbers, and may still be consulted by those who are able to read them.

It looks as if it were the policy of the Benedictines to give as many monks as possible some special duty and responsibility—to give each, in fact, a personal interest in the prosperity of the house to which he belonged—and the vacancies occurring from time to time in the various offices gave everybody something to look forward to. There was room for ambition, and, I am bound to add, room for a good deal of petty scheming, on the one hand, and truckling to the abbot, on the other; but it all went towards relieving the monotony of the life in the cloister—a monotony which has been very much over-stated by those who have never studied the subject. To begin with, it does not follow that what would be very dull to us would be dull and insipid to the men of the thirteenth century. Before a man offered himself for admission to a monastery, he must have had a taste for a quiet life, and in many instances he had grown tired of the bustle, the struggle, and all the anxious wear of the work-day world. He wanted to be rid of *bothers*, in fact; he was pretty sure to have had a fair education, and he was presumably a religious man, with a taste for religious exercises; sometimes, and not unfrequently, he was a disappointed man, who had been left wifeless and childless; sometimes, too, he was one whose career had been cut short suddenly by some accident which incapacitated him for active exertion and made him long only for repose and obscurity. Moreover, in those distant times the instinct of devotion was incomparably stronger than it is now, and people found a real and intense delight in the services of the sanctuary, to say nothing of their entire belief in the spiritual advantages to be derived from taking part in those services. Add to this that a monk had to pass through rather a long training before he was regularly admitted to full membership. He had to submit to a term of probation, during which he was subject to a somewhat rigorous ordeal.

A novice had the pride taken out of him in a very effectual way during his novitiate—he was pretty much in the position of a *fag* at a great school nowadays, and by the time that he had passed through his novitiate he was usually very well broken in, and in harmony with the spirit of the place in which he found himself. It was something to have a higher place assigned him at last in the church and the dormitory, to have some petty office given him, and to have a chance of being promoted by and by. There was Brother So-and-so, who was getting infirm, and he could not do the pitanciar's work much longer; the precentor was getting as hoarse as a raven, and the sacrist was gouty, or the cellarer was showing signs of breaking up. Nay, the prior's cough gave unmistakable signs of his lungs being wrong, and if he *were* to drop off, which we should of course all of us deplore—there would be a general move up, it might be; unless, indeed, Father Abbot should promote his chaplain over the heads of all of us—for such things have been!

But, when we come to look a little closer, we find that the monotony of monastic life was almost confined to the frequent services in the church. There were six services every day, of one kind or another, at which the whole convent was supposed to be present, and one service at midnight.[1] The lay brethren among the Cistercians, and the servants engaged in field labour, were excused attendance at the nocturnal service, and those officials of the convent whose business required them to be absent from the precincts were also excused. Indeed, it would have been simply impossible for the whole brotherhood to assemble at all these services; there would have been a dead-lock in twenty-four hours if the attempt had ever been made in any of the large monasteries, where the inmates sometimes counted by hundreds, who all expected their meals punctually, and for whom even the simplest cookery necessitated that fires should be kept up, the porridge boiled, the beer drawn, and the bread baked. Hence, they whose hands were full and their engagements many really had no time to put in an appearance at church seven times in twenty-four hours. While, on the other hand, the monk out of office, with nothing particular to do, was all the better for having his time broken up; going to church kept him out of mischief, and singing of psalms saved him from idle talk, and

[1] Peckham's Register, ii., Preface, p. lxviii. et seq.

if it did him no good certainly did him very little harm.

The ordinary life of the monastery began at six o'clock in the morning, and when the small bell, called the skilla, rang, all rose, washed themselves at the latrines, put on their day habit, and then presented themselves at the matin Mass. *Mixtum*, or breakfast, followed, and that over the convent assembled in chapter for consultation. After chapter the officials dispersed ; the kitchener to arrange for the meals, and not unfrequently to provide hospitality for distinguished guests and their retinue ; the precentor to drill his choir boys, to tune the organ, to look after the music, or to arrange for some procession in the church, or some extraordinary function ; the infirmarer to take his rounds in the hospital ; the cellarer to inspect the brewhouse and bakeries ; and each or all of these officers might find it necessary to go far a-field in looking after some bailiff or tenant who could not safely be left alone. At Evesham the sacristan, the chamberlain, and the infirmarer were allowed forage and the keep of one horse. Meanwhile in the cloister all was stir and movement without noise. In the west alley the schoolmaster was teaching his little pupils the rudiments of Latin, or it might be the elements of singing ; in the south alley, where the light was best, a monk with a taste for art was trying his hand at illuminating a MS. or rubricating the initial letters; while on the other side, in the north alley, some were painfully getting by heart the psalms, or practising meditation—alone in a crowd.

Within the retirement of that cloister, fenced all round, as I have said, with the high walls and the great buildings, there the monks were working, there the real conventual life was going on; but outside the cloister, though yet within the precincts, it is difficult for us now to realize what a vast hive of industry a great monastery in some of the lonely and thinly-populated parts of England was. Everything that was eaten or drunk or worn, almost everything that was made or used in a monastery, was produced upon the spot. The grain grew on their own land; the corn was ground in their own mill; their clothes were made from the wool of their own sheep; they had their own tailors and shoemakers, and carpenters and blacksmiths, almost within call; they kept their own bees; they grew their own garden-stuff and their own fruit; I suspect they knew more of fish-culture than, until very lately, we moderns could boast of knowing. Nay, they had their own vineyards and made their own wine.

The commissariat of a large abbey must have required administrative ability of a very high order, and the cost of hospitality was enormous. No traveller, whatever his degree, was refused food and shelter, and every monastery was a vast hotel, where nobody need pay more than he chose for his board and lodging. The mere keeping the accounts must have employed no small number of clerks, for the minuteness with which every transaction was recorded, almost passes belief. Those rolls I spoke of—the sacrist's, cellarer's, and so on—were, it must be remembered, periodical balance-sheets handed in at audit day. They deal, not only with pence and half-pence, but with farthings and half-farthings, and were compiled from the tablets or small account-books posted up from day to day and hour to hour. They give the price of every nail hammered into a wall, and rarely omit the cost of the parchment on which the roll itself is written. The men must have been very busy, or, if you prefer it, very fussy—certainly they could not have been idle to have kept their accounts in this painfully minute manner, even to the fraction of a farthing.

* * * * * *

In the natural course of events, as a monastery grew in wealth and importance, there was one element of interest which added great zest to the conventual life, in the *quarrels* that were sure to arise.

First and foremost, the most desirable person to

quarrel with was a Bishop. In its original idea, a monastery was not necessarily an ecclesiastical institution. It was not necessary that an abbot should be an ecclesiastic, and not essentially necessary that any one of his monks should be in holy orders. Long before the thirteenth century, however, a monk was almost invariably ordained, and being an ordained person, and having his local habitation in a bishop's diocese, it was only natural that the bishop should claim jurisdiction over him and over the church in which he and the fraternity ministered; but to allow a power of visitation to any one outside the close corporation of the convent was fraught with infinite peril to the community. Confessing their faults one to another, and asking pardon of the Lord Abbot or his representative, the prior, was one thing; but to have a querulous or inquisitive or even hostile bishop coming and intruding into their secrets, blurting them out to the world and actually pronouncing sentence upon them—that seemed to the monks an absolutely intolerable and shocking condition of affairs. Hence it seemed supremely desirable to a convent to get for itself, by fair means or foul—and I am afraid the means were not always fair means, as we should consider them—the exemption of their house from episcopal visitation or control. I believe that the earliest instance of such an exemption being granted

in England was that of the Conqueror's Abbey of
Battle. The precedent was a bad one, and led to all
sorts of attempts by other houses to procure for
themselves the like privilege. Such attempts were
stoutly resisted by the bishops, who foresaw the evils
that would inevitably follow, and which in fact did
follow ; and, of course, bishop and abbey went to law.
Going to law in this case meant usually, first, a
certain amount of preliminary litigation before the
Archbishop of Canterbury ; but sooner or later it
was sure to end in an appeal to the Pope's court, or,
as the phrase was, an appeal to Rome.

Without wishing for a moment to defend or excuse
a state of things which was always vexatious, and at
last became intolerable, it is impossible to deny that
a great deal of nonsense has been talked and written
about these appeals. Almost exactly the same state
of things exists in the present day both in civil and
ecclesiastical matters. Parsee merchants fall to
loggerheads in Bombay or Calcutta, and bring their
disputes before the courts in India ; one side feels
aggrieved by the sentence, and straightway he re-
moves the case to a court of appeal in London. Or
some heretical person in Asia or Africa or somewhere
else gets into hot water with an orthodox society for
the promotion of religious persecution, and sooner or
later the archbishop is appealed to, and the ecclesias-

tical lawyers have a most delightful time of it. It all costs a great deal of money nowadays, and leading advocates on this side or that are actually so extortionate and exorbitant that they will not do anything for nothing, and insist on receiving the most exorbitant fees. So it was in the old days. The final court of appeal in all matters ecclesiastical was before the Pope at Rome or Avignon, and the proctors and doctors, and all the canonists and officials, actually required to be paid for their work.

When a monastery was in for a great fight with a bishop, it was a serious matter for both parties. But it was much more serious for the bishop than for the convent. The bishop had always his state to keep up and his many houses to maintain, and his establishment was enormously costly. His margin for law expenses was small ; and I suspect that a bishop in England during the thirteenth century who had no private fortune outside his mere episcopal revenues would have been likely sooner or later to find himself in serious difficulties. On the other hand, in a great monastery all sorts of expedients could be resorted to in order to effect a salutary retrenchment—as when the monks of St. Alban's agreed to give up the use of wine for fifteen years, and actually did so, that they might be able to rebuild their refectory and dormitory in the days of John the twenty-first abbot. Moreover, inasmuch as a corporation never dies, the convent could raise very heavy sums on the security of its estates, and take its own time to repay the loans. A bishop could not pledge his episcopal estates beyond his own lifetime, and the result was that, in the days when life assurance was unknown, a bishop who had to raise money for a costly lawsuit would have to pay a rate of interest which would make our blood run cold if we had to pay it, or our hearts leap for joy if we could get it in these days of two and three per cent. The bishop was always at a disadvantage in these appeal cases; he stood to lose everything, and he stood to win nothing at all except the satisfaction of his conscience that he was struggling for principle and right. And thus it came to pass that the monks enjoyed this kind of warfare, and rarely shrank from engaging in it. Indeed, an appeal to Rome meant sending a deputation from the convent to watch the case as it was going on, and there was all the delight of a foreign tour an a sight of the world—a trip, in fact, to the Continent at the expense of the establishment.

But when there was no appeal case going on—and an appeal was too expensive an amusement to be indulged in often—there was always a good deal of exciting litigation to keep up the interest of the convent, and to give them something to think about and gossip about nearer home. We have the best authority—the authority of the great Pope Innocent III.—for believing that Englishmen in the thirteenth century were extremely fond of beer; but there was something else that they were even fonder of, and that was law. Monastic history is almost made up of the stories of this everlasting litigation; nothing was too trifling to be made into an occasion for a lawsuit. Some neighbouring landowner had committed a trespass or withheld a tithe pig. Some audacious townsman had claimed the right of catching eels in a pond. Some brawling knight pretended he was in some sense *patron* of a cell, and demanded a trumpery allowance of bread and ale, or an equivalent. As we read about these things we exclaim, " Why in the world did they make such a fuss about a trifle ? " Not so thought the monks. They knew well enough what the thin end of the wedge meant, and, being in a far better position than we are to judge of the significance and importance of many a *casus belli* which now seems but trivial, they never dreamed of giving an inch for the other side to take an ell. So they went to law, and enjoyed it amazingly! Sometimes however, there were disputes which were not to be settled peaceably; and then came what University men in the old days used to know as a " Town and Gown row."

Let it be remembered that a Benedictine monastery, in the early times, was invariably set down in a lonely wilderness. As time went on, and the monks brought the swamp into cultivation, and wealth flowed in, and the monastery became a centre of culture, there would be sure to gather round the walls a number of hangers-on, who gradually grew into a community, the tendency of which was to assert itself, and to become less and less dependent upon the abbey for support. These *towns* (for they became such) were, as a rule, built on the abbey land, and paid dues to the monastery. Of course, on the one side, there was an inclination to raise the dues; on the other, a desire to repudiate them altogether. Hence bad blood was sure to arise between the monks and the townsmen, and sooner or later serious conflicts between the servants of the monasteries and the people outside. Thus, in 1223, there was a serious collision between the Londoners and the Westminster monks; the mob rushed into the monastery, and the abbot escaped their violence with difficulty by slipping out at a back door and getting into a boat on the Thames. On another occasion there was a very serious fray between the citizens of Norwich and the priory there, in 1272, when the prior slew one man with his own hands, and many lives were lost. At a later time there was a similar disturbance at Bury St. Edmunds, and in the year 1314 the great abbey of St. Alban's was kept in a state of siege for more than ten days by the townsmen, who were driven to frenzy by not being allowed to grind their own corn in their own handmills, but compelled to get it ground by the abbey millers, and, of course, pay the fee.

Thirty years later, again, that man of sin, Sir Philip de Lymbury, lifted up his heel against the Abbey of St. Alban's, and actually laid hands upon Brother John Moot, the cellarer; and on Monday, being market day at Luton in Beds, did actually clap the said cellarer in the pillory, and kept him there, exposed to the jeers and contempt of the rude populace, who, we may be sure, were in ecstasies at this precursor of Mr. Pickwick in the pound. But the holy martyr St. Alban was not likely to let such an outrage pass; and when the rollicking knight came to the abbey to make it up, and was for presenting a peace-offering at the shrine, lo, the knightly nose began to bleed profusely, and, to the consternation of the beholders, the offering could not be made, and Sir Philip had to retire, holding his nose, and shortly after he died—and, adds the chronicler, was speedily forgotten, he and his.

Such ruffling of the peace and quiet of conventual life was, there is reason to believe, not uncommon. But inside the cloister itself there was not always a holy calm. When the abbot died there came all the canvassing and excitement of a contested election, and sometimes a convent might be turned for years into a house divided against itself, the two parties among the monks fighting like cat and dog. Nor did it at all follow that because the convent had elected their abbot or prior unanimously that therefore the election was allowed by the king, to whom the elect was presented.[1] King John kept monasteries without any abbot for years, sequestrating the estates in the meantime, and leaving the monks to make the best of it. Sometimes an abbot was forced upon a monastery in spite of the convent, as in the case of Abbot Roger Norreys at Evesham, in 1191—a man whom the monks not only detested because of his gross mismanagement, but whom they denounced as actually immoral. Sometimes, too, the misconduct of a prior was so abominable that it could not be borne, and then came the very difficult and very delicate business of getting him deposed : a process which was by no means easily managed, as appeared in the instance of Simon Pumice, Prior of Worcester, in 1219, and in many another case.

Such hopes and fears and provocations as these all contributed to relieve the monotony which it has

[1] See a notable instance in Carlyle's " Past and Present."

been too readily assumed was the characteristic of the cloister life. The monks had a world of their own within the precincts, but they were not so shut in but that their relations with the greater world outside were very real. Moreover, that confinement to the monastery itself, which was necessarily very greatly relaxed in the case of the officers or obedientaries of the convent, was almost as easily relaxed if one of the brethren could manage to get the right side of the abbot or prior. When Archbishop Peckham was holding his visitations in 1282 he more than once remarks with asperity upon a monk *farming* a manor of his convent, and declares that the practice must stop. The outlying manors must have somebody to look after them, it was assumed, and if one of the brethren was willing to undertake the management for the convent, why should he not ?

Nor, again, must we suppose that the monks were debarred all amusements. On August 29, 1283, there was a great wrestling match at Hockliffe, in Beds, and a huge concourse of people of all sorts were there to see the fun. The roughs and the " fancy " were present in great force, and somehow it came to pass that a free fight ensued. I am sorry to say that the canons of Dunstable were largely represented upon the occasion. We are left to infer

F

that the representatives were chiefly the servants of the canons, but I am afraid that *some* at least of their masters were there too. In the fight one Simon Mustard, who appears to have been something like a professional prize-fighter, "a bully exceeding fierce," says the annalist, got killed; but thereon ensued much inquiry and much litigation, and Dunstable and its "religious" had to suffer vexations not a few. In fairness it should be remembered that these Dunstable people were not monks but canons—regular or irregular—and those canons, we all know, would do anything. We protest against being confounded with canons!

The amusements of monks were more innocent. The garden was always a great place of resort, and gardening a favourite pastime. We may be sure there was much lamentation and grumbling at St. Alban's when Abbot John de Maryns forbade any monk, who from infirmity could only be carried on a litter, from entering the garden at all. Poor old fellows! had their bearers been disorderly and trodden upon the flower-beds? Bowls was the favourite and a very common diversion among them; but in the opinion of Archbishop Peckham, as appears by his letters, there were other diversions of a far more reprehensible character. Actually at the small Priory of Coxford, in Norfolk, the prior and his canons were wholly given over to chess-playing. It was dreadful! In other monasteries the monks positively hunted; not only the abbots, but the common domestic monks! Nay, such things were to be found as monks keeping dogs, or even birds, in the cloister. Peckham denounces these breaches of decorum as grave offences, which were not to be passed over and not to be allowed. What! a black monk stalking along with a bull-pup at his heels, and a jackdaw, worse than the Jackdaw of Rheims, using bad words in the garth, and showing an evil example to the chorister boys, with his head on one side!

But, after all, it must be confessed that the greatest of all delights to the thirteenth-century monks was eating and drinking. " Sir, I like my dinner! " said Dr. Johnson, and I don't think any one thought the worse of him for his honest outspokenness. The dinner in a great abbey was clearly a very important event in the day—I will not say it was *the* important event, but it was a *very* important one. It must strike any one who knows much of the literature of this age that the weak point in the monastic life of the thirteenth century was the gormandizing. It was exactly as, I am told, it is on board ship on a long voyage, where people have little or nothing to do, they are always looking forward to the next meal, and the sound of the dinner-bell is the most exciting

sound that greets the ear in the twenty-four hours.
And so with the monks in a great monastery which
had grown rich, and in point of fact had more money
than it knew what to do with: the dinner was the
event of the day. It is not that we hear much of
drunkenness, for we really hear very little of it, and
where it is spoken of it is always with reprobation.
Nor is it that we hear of anything like the loathsome
and disgusting gluttony of the Romans of the empire,
but eating and drinking, and especially eating, are
always cropping up; one is perpetually being reminded of them in one way or another, and it is
significant that when the Cistercian revival began,
one of the chief reforms aimed at was the rigorous
simplification of the meals and the curtailing the
luxury of the refectory.

But the monks were not the only people in those
times who had a high appreciation of good cheer.
When a man of high degree took up his quarters in
a monastery he by no means wished to be put off
with salt-fish-and-toast-and-water cheer. Richard
de Marisco, one of King John's profligate councillors,
who was eventually foisted into the see of Dur-
ham, gave the Abbey of St. Alban's the tithes of
Eglingham, in Northumberland, to help them to
make their ale better—" taking compassion upon the
weakness of the convent's drink," as the chronicler

tells us. The small beer of St. Alban's, it seems, was not so much improved as was to be desired, notwithstanding this appropriation of Church property, for twice after this the abbey had the same delicate hint given to it that its brewing was not up to the mark, when the rectory of Norton, in Hertfordshire, and two-thirds of the tithes of Hartburn, in Northumberland, were given to the monastery that no excuse might remain for the bad quality of the malt liquor.

And here let me remark in passing that another wide-spread delusion needs to be removed from the popular mind with regard to the relations between the monks and the clergy. We have again and again heard people say, " Wonderfully devoted men, those monks! Look at the churches all over the land! If it had not been for the monks how could all the village churches have been built? The monks built them all!" Monks build parish churches! Why, the monks were always robbing the country parsons, and the town parsons, too, for that matter. Every vicarage in England represents a spoliation of the church, whose rectorial tithes had been appropriated by a religious house, the parson being left with the vicarial tithes, and often not even with them, but thrown for his daily bread upon the

voluntary offerings of his parishioners. The monks
build churches ! I could not from my own knowledge
bring forward a single instance in all the history of
— England of a monastery contributing a shilling of
money or a load of stone for the repair, let alone the
erection, of any parish church in the land. So far
from it, they pulled down the churches when they
had a chance, and they were always on the look-out
to steal the rectory houses and substitute for them
any cheap-and-nasty vicarage unless the bishop kept
a sharp look-out upon them and came to the help of
his clergy. Of all the sins that the monks had to
answer for, this greedy grasping at Church property,
this shameless robbery of the seculars, was beyond
compare the most inexcusable and the most mischievous. To the credit of the Cistercians it must
be told that they *at first* set themselves against the
wholesale pillage of the parochial clergy. I am not
prepared to say they were true to their first principles
—no corporate society ever was, and least of all a
religious corporation—but at starting the Cistercians
were decidedly opposed to the alienating of tithes and
appropriating them to the endowment of their abbeys,
and this was probably one among other causes why
the Cistercians prospered so wonderfully as they did
during the first hundred years or so after their first
coming here ; people believed that the new order was

not going to live by robbing parsons, as the older orders had done without remorse. The swindler always thinks his victim a fool, and the victim never forgives the smarter man who has taken him in. Accordingly the monks always pretended to think scorn of the clergy, and when the monasteries fell the clergy were the very last people to lament their fall.

And this brings us to the question of the moral condition of the monasteries. Bishop Stubbs has called the thirteenth century " the golden age of English Churchmanship." Subject to correction from the greatest of England's great historians—and subject to correction, too, from others, who, standing in a rank below his unapproachable eminence, are yet very much my superiors in their knowledge of this subject—I venture to express my belief that the thirteenth century was also the golden age of English Monachism. Certainly we know much more about the monasteries and their inner life during this period than at any other time. The materials ready to our hand are very voluminous, and the evidence accessible to the inquirer is very various. I do not believe that any man of common fairness and candour who should give some years to the careful study of those materials and that evidence could rise from his examination with any other impression than

that, as a body, the monks of the thirteenth century
were better than their age. Vicious and profligate,
drunken and unchaste, as a class, they certainly were
not. Of course there were scandalous brethren.
Here and there—but rarely, very rarely—there was
a wicked abbot or prior. Of course there were
instances of abominations on which one cannot
dwell ; of course there are stories which are bad to
read ; stories which find their way into the chronicles
because they were strange or startling ; but these
stories are always told with horror, and commented
upon with severity and scorn. Excuse for wickedness or any palliation of it, you simply never find.

On the other hand, the intense *esprit de corps* of a
convent of monks went beyond anything that we
can now realize, and led to grave sins against truth
and honesty. The forgeries of charters, bulls, and
legal instruments of all kinds for the glorification of
a monastery by its members was at least condoned
only too frequently. It can hardly be doubted that
the scriptorium of many a religious house must have
been turned to very discreditable uses by unscrupulous and clever scribes, with the connivance if not
with the actual knowledge of the convent, for such
things were not done in a corner. If the forgeries succeeded—and that they often did succeed we know—
the monastery got all the advantage of the rascality ;

no inquiry was made, and it was tacitly assumed that where so much was gained, and the pride of "our house" was gratified, the end justified the means.

There remains one question which may suggest itself to our minds as it has often suggested itself to others. From what class or classes in society were the monks for the most part taken? This is one of the most difficult questions to answer. The late Dr. Maitland, who perhaps knew more, and had read more, about monks and monasteries than any Englishman of his time, professed himself unable to answer it; and my friend Dr. Luard—whose labours in this field of research have gained for him a European reputation, and whose wonderful industry, carefulness, and profound knowledge, qualify him to speak with authority on such a point, if any one might pronounce upon it—hesitates to give a decided opinion. The impression that is left upon my own mind is, that the thirteenth-century monk, as a rule, was drawn from the gentry class, as distinguished from the aristocracy on the one hand, or the artisans on the other. In fact, *mutatis mutandis*, that the representatives of the monks of the thirteenth century were the Fellows of Colleges of the nineteenth before the recent alteration of University and College statutes came into force. An ignorant monk was certainly a rarity, an absolutely unlettered or uneducated one was an impossibility, and an abbot or prior who could not talk and write Latin with facility, who could not preach with tolerable fluency on occasion, and hold his own as a debater and man of business, would have found himself sooner or later in a very ridiculous and very uncomfortable position, from which he might be glad to escape by resignation.

.   .   .   .   .   .

Three centuries after the time we have been considering, the religious houses were suppressed—to use that euphonious term which has become universally accepted—only after they had existed in these islands in one form or another for at least a thousand years. Century after century monasteries continued to spring up, and there never was much difficulty in finding devout people who were ready to befriend a new order, to endow it with lands, and to give it a fair start. In other words, there was always a *demand* for new monasteries; and the first sure sign that that demand had been met, and more than met, was when the supply of monks began to fall short, and when, as was the case before the end of the fifteenth century, the religious houses could not fill up their full complement of brethren. Is it conceivable that this constant demand could have gone on, unless the common sense of the nation had been profoundly convinced, and continuously convinced, that the religious orders gave back some great equivalent for all the immense surrenders of wealth which generation after generation of Englishmen had made—some equivalent for all the vast stream of benefactions which flowed on from age to age so strongly that kings and statesmen had to interfere and check, if it might be, the dangerous prodigality of lavish benefactors? What that equivalent was, what the real work of the monasteries was, what great functions they discharged in the body politic, what the nation at large gained by their continuance and lost by their fall—these are questions which on this occasion I am not concerned with, and with which I scrupulously forbear from dealing. But there are moments when a great horror comes upon some men's minds, and a vision of a lonely and childless old age rises before them in the gloom of a dreary twilight, or when the mists of autumn hide the sunbeams, and they think, " If desolation were to come upon our homes, where could we hide the stricken head and broken heart?" To that question —a morbid question if you will—I have never found an answer The answer was possible once, but it was in an age which has passed away.

Yes, that age has passed away for ever. History

repeats itself, it is true, but history will not bear mimicry. In every melody that wakes the echoes there is repetition of this note and that, the same single sound is heard again and again; but the glorious intertwinings of the several parts, the subtle fugues and merry peals of laughter that "flash along the chords and go," the wail of the minor, as if crying for the theme that has vanished and yet will reappear —" like armies whispering where great echoes be "— these things are not mere repetition; they are messages from the Eternal Father to the sons of men, reminding them that the world moves on. Merely to ape the past, and to attempt to reproduce in the nineteenth century the tree that had taken a millennium to grow into its maturity in the thirteenth and was rudely cut down root and branch in the sixteenth, is about as wise as it would be to try and make us sing the Hallelujah Chorus in unison! Let the dead bury their dead.

Meanwhile the successors of the thirteenth-century monasteries are rising up around us each after his kind; Pall Mall swarms with them, hardly less splendid than their progenitors, certainly not less luxurious. Our modern monks look out at the windows of the Carlton and the Athenæum with no suspicion that they are at all like the monks of old. Nor are they. They lack the old faith, the old loyalty to their order, and with the old picturesqueness something else that we can less afford to miss—the old enthusiasm. We look back upon the men of the thirteenth century with much complacency. A supercilious glance at the past seems to give the moderns an excellent opinion of themselves. But suppose the men of the thirteenth century could turn the tables upon us, and, from their point of view, pass their judgment upon the daily life of the conventuals of St. James's, who are, after all, only survivals, but just conceivably not quite survivals of the fittest; would the monks of old find all things quite up to the highest ideal, or would they hide their heads in shame and confusion of face compelled to acknowledge that the new is in all things so much better than the old?

IV.

THE BLACK DEATH IN EAST ANGLIA.

> " So they died ! The dead were slaying the dying,
>   And a famine of strivers silenced strife :
>   There were none to love and none to wed,
>   And pity and joy and hope had fled,
>   And grief had spent her passion in sighing ;
>   And where was the Spirit of Life ? "

FROM across the Channel during the last few
months [1] there have come to us tidings of a visitation
of pestilence which have seemed to some men very
disquieting, and to some heavy with menace. From
Italy, the land beyond the Alps ; from Spain, the
land beyond the Pyrenees ; from seaports in France
and cities of the plain, we hear that the cholera has
been striking down its victims. The Phantom with
the deadly breath has shown strange caprice in his
coming and going ; but when he has been suspected
to be nigh at hand, wild-eyed Panic has shown herself as of old. It is sad and discouraging to find that,

[1] February, 1884.

166

spite of all our boasted progress—all that science has taught us, and all that we are supposed to have learnt—the attitude of the multitude when certain dangers threaten, appears to be as it was, and that we still hear of shuddering wretches trying to fight a dreaded enemy by letting off old muskets and drenching portmanteaus with Condy's fluid.

Such things have been before. Must they recur again? Philosophers comfort us with the assurance that our brains are larger than those of our forefathers. Nay, that the convolutions of the said brains are more complex. How about the *moral fibre?* Are we never to have stouter hearts or more "bowels and mercies?" In the face of the same circumstances, will men for ever show themselves the same? Or is it that all these stories of mad stampedes and of chaotic anarchy breaking loose here and there—anarchy gibbering, blind, profligate and senselessly cruel—are true only of exceptional communities, as yet unaffected by the great lift which optimists confidently believe in, and which they unhesitatingly assure us is steadily going on?

The cholera has abated, we are told; as we were told it would. Thus far we in England have escaped its ravages. Experts—and experts are the people whose vocation it is to speak without doubt or hesitation whenever they speak—experts assure us that London was never more free from cholera than during this present summer. Other experts—they too speaking with authority—confidently affirm that our time is coming, that a severe visitation is impending; that all we have heard of hitherto of the ravages of the epidemic elsewhere, will prove but child's play in comparison with that which we shall hear of by and by. "And then, sir, you'll see!" That is a comforting assurance—at any rate, *some* of us will survive.

But what do we know of the march of any mysterious form of death that has ever appeared in bygone ages, suddenly starting up and striding over the earth—"the land as a garden of Eden before him, and behind him a desolate wilderness?" We have most of us read of such frightful visitations in Thucydides, in Ovid, in Virgil, in Lucretius, not to mention the moderns; but if any of us were to write down the sum and substance of his knowledge, and attempt to discover from any trustworthy evidence the nature, the course, and the intensity of any great plague that has ever proved a real scourge upon any large section of the human race, what would his summing-up amount to? How long would it take to write; or rather, when it was written, how long would it take to read?

This island of Great Britain has more than once

been visited by pestilence. De Foe has left us an inimitable romance, which he calls " The History of the Plague in London in 1665." How much or how little of sober fact there may be in those thrilling incidents, worked up so marvellously by the great novelist, it is impossible to say. That there is at least as much of fiction as of fact in the book none can doubt. The author was a child when the plague was raging—a child of two years' old, toddling about the butcher's shop. The plague of 1665 did not travel far ; out of London its incidence was comparatively trifling. The cholera has visited us again and again, but never on a scale to demoralize the people at large. Only once in our history has the destroyer passed over England, leaving probably no shire unvisited by his awful presence, and no parish in which there was not one dead. It is never fair to draw inferences from the silence of historians ; but it is at least significant that among all contemporary writers who have made mention of the Black Death—as it has been agreed to call it—the Black Death in the reign of Edward III.—there is little mention of any panic, few ugly tales of desertion of the dying, no flagrant instances of miserable creatures crying that the wells were poisoned. On the contrary, we have proof that as a rule men died at their posts during all that trying time, that those in authority never lost their heads, and that though there must, of course, have been isolated cases of abject fear, expressing itself in the maddest extravagances of despair, yet we have to look long and look far and wide to find such cases—and after all our search may be fruitless.

As yet the history of the Black Death can hardly be said to have been investigated at all; and until specialists can be prevailed upon to examine the evidence ready at hand, we shall continue to be put off with mere generalities when we ask for more light upon a calamity which was the most stupendous that ever befell this island.

.   .   .   .   .   .

We have all heard of Boccaccio's *Decameron*—only naughty people have *read* it—and how it was written when the plague was raging at Florence, the great plague that carried off Petrarch's Laura, and those other thousands of whom the world knew nothing then and knows nothing now. Some, too, have heard that the plague swept over Europe—desolating, devastating—the spectre with the swinging scythe mowing down broad swathes of men. Some, when they hear of it, picture to themselves Pope Clement VI. at Avignon, sitting in that vast palace that overlooks the Rhone, the stench of corpses mastered for him by the fragrant smoke of aromatic logs burning in huge pyres round about him night and day. Some have heard of Giovanne Villani, the historian of Florence, who wrote feebly about that same pestilence in his native city, and who doubtless would have written more, and more plainly and more strongly, but that in the midst of his writing Azrael touched him too, and his pen fell from his hand.[1] Some few, again, have a faint recollection of that Emperor of the West, John Cantacuzene, who ruled at Constantinople when the plague was, and who wrote about it.[2] Didn't he? Nay! Hadn't he a son, Andronicus, who died of it? How did it come to pass that Gibbon did not so much as allude to it? Some, peradventure, think of Rome and of Rienzi, and how it was about that time that he was potent, or was he in hiding there among the Fraticelli? And isn't there something too about the plague visiting Greenland, and putting back the clock that was moving on steadily, but which suddenly stopped? How vague we are!

. . . . . .

What was this plague? How did it strike men down?

"It showed itself," says Boccaccio, "in a sad and

---

[1] Muratori, "Rerum Italicarum Scriptores," vol. xiii. pp. 1–771.

[2] His four books of Histories are to be found in the "Corpus Scriptorum Historiæ Byzantinæ."

wonderful manner; and *different from what it had
been in the East,* where bleeding from the nose is the
fatal prognostic, here [at Florence] there appeared
certain tumours in the groin or under the armpits,
some as big as an apple, others as big as an egg;
and afterwards purple spots in most parts of the
body: in some cases large and but few in number,
in others less and more numerous, both kinds the
usual messengers of death. . . . They generally
died," he adds, "the third day from the first appearance of the symptoms, without a fever or other bad
circumstance attending."

"It took men generally in the head and stomach,
appearing first in the groin," says Villani, "or under
the armpits, by little knobs or swellings called
kernels, boils, blains, blisters, pimples, or plague-
sores; being generally attended with devouring fever,
with occasional spitting and vomiting of blood,
whence, for the most part, they died presently
or in half a day, or within a day or two at the
most."

Less precise and minute is the description of the
great surgeon, Guido de Chauliac, who nobly stayed
at Avignon for the six months during which the
visitation was at its worst; but he too mentions the
carbuncular swellings in the axillæ and the groin,

the purple spots, and the violent inflammation of the lungs, attended by fatal expectoration of blood.

As for the Emperor John Cantacuzene, his description is so flagrantly a mere adaptation of the history of the plague at Athens by Thucydides that it must be received with caution. It is only in what it omits and in what it adds to the older narrative that it possesses any great historic value. It agrees with the accounts quoted above in making mention of the swellings, the blood-spitting, and the awful rapidity with which the disease ran its course. It omits all mention of the eruption on the surface of the skin, the flushed eyes, and, above all, the swollen and inflamed condition of the larynx, the cough, the sneezing, and the hiccough, which Dr. Collier found so significant.

Comparing, then, the several accounts which have come down to us, meagre though they are, it ought to be possible to arrive at some conclusions regarding the nature of the plague of the fourteenth century which, for the pathologist, would amount to certainties. The wonder is that such men as Dr. Hecker and his learned translator should have shown so much reserve—not to say timidity—in pronouncing judgment upon the question.

A layman runs a risk of incurring withering scorn at his presumption, and ridicule at his ignorance who ventures to express an opinion—or to have one—on any subject which the medical profession claims as within its own domain ; and I should not dare to speak otherwise than as a very humble inquirer when the learned are silent. There are, however, some conclusions which may be accepted without hesitation and which will be admitted by all.

I. The Black Death was *not* scarlatina maligna, as the plague at Athens undoubtedly was.[1]

II. It was *not* small-pox.

III. It was *not* cholera.

IV. It probably *was* a variety of the Oriental plague, which has reappeared in Europe in more modern times, and regarding which they who wish to know more must seek their information where it is to be found.

The next question usually asked is, Where did the new plague come from ? And here the answer is even more uncertain than that to the other question —What the great plague was.

In fact, a careful comparison of such testimony as comes to hand leaves the inquirer in a very perplexed condition, and inclines him rather to accept than reject the old-fashioned theory of a " general corruption of the atmosphere " as the only working hypothesis whereby to account for the startling sponta-

[1] " The History of the Plague of Athens," translated from Thucydides by C. Collier, M.D.   London, 1857.

neity of the outbreak and its appearance at so many and such distant points at the same time.

The Imperial author, who appears to have done his best to gather information, evidently found himself quite baffled in his attempt to follow the march of the plague. It had originated among the Hyperborean Scythians; it had passed through Pontus, and Libya, and Syria, and the furthest East, and "in a manner all the world round about." Other writers are just as much in the dark as Cantacuzene, and it seems mere waste of time to endeavour to arrive at any conclusion from data so defective and statements so void of historical basis as have come down to us. This only seems established, that during the year 1347 there was great atmospheric disturbance extending over a large area of Southern Europe, and resulting in extensive failure of the harvest, and consequent distress and famine; and that in January, 1348, one of the most violent earthquakes in history wrought immense havoc in Italy, the shocks being felt in the islands of the Mediterranean, and even north of the Alps.

It is at least curious that the date of the earthquake coincides very closely with the date which has been given by Guido de Chauliac for the first appearance of the plague at Avignon. He tells us expressly that it broke out in that city in January, 1348, and

I think it would be difficult to produce trustworthy evidence of any earlier outbreak than this, at any rate, in Europe.[1] "It appeared at Florence," says Villani, "at the beginning of April, and at Cesena, on the other side of the Apennines, on the 1st of June." It is asserted that it reached England at the beginning of August, is said to have lingered for some months in the west, and to have devastated Bristol with awful severity.

There can be no doubt that in the towns of Italy and France there was a dreadful mortality; but when we are told that 100,000 died in Venice, and 60,000 in Florence, and 70,000 in Siena, it is impossible to accept such round numbers as anything better than ignorant guesses. Whether the great cities of the Low Countries were visited by the pestilence with any severity, or how far the towns of Germany were affected, I am unable to say, nor am I much concerned at present with such an inquiry; that I leave to others to throw light upon. But as to the progress, the incidence, and the effect of the Black Death in England—when it came and where it showed itself, how long it lasted, and what

[1] One of our monastic chroniclers states expressly that it began about St. James's Day in 1347. I *feel* certain that the date is wrong, and that it could be proved to be wrong without much difficulty by reference to documentary evidence which might be consulted.

effects followed—on these questions the time has come for pointing out that we have a body of evidence such as perhaps exists in no other country —evidence, too, which hitherto has hardly received any attention, its very existence entirely overlooked, forgotten, nay! not even suspected.

. . . . . .

Let us understand where we are, and look about us for a little while.

When King Edward III. entered London in triumph on the 14th of October, 1347, he was the foremost man in Europe, and England had reached a height of power and glory such as she had never attained before. At the battle of Creçi France had received a crushing blow, and by the loss of Calais, after an eleven months' siege, she had been reduced well-nigh to the lowest point of humiliation. David II., King of Scotland, was now lying a prisoner in the Tower of London. Louis of Bavaria had just been killed by a fall from his horse, the Imperial throne was vacant, and the electors in eager haste proclaimed that they had chosen the King of England to succeed. To their discomfiture the King of England declined the proffered crown. He "had other views." Intoxicated by the splendour of their sovereign and his martial renown, and the success which seemed to attend him wherever he showed himself, the English people had gone mad with exultation—all except the merchant princes, the monied men, who are not often given to lose their heads. They took a much more sober view of the outlook than the populace did—they had an eye to their own interests and the interests of the trade and commerce in which they were engaged. They were very much in earnest in asserting their rights and protesting against their wrongs, and they presented their petitions to the King after the fashion of the time—petitions which must have seemed rather startling protests in the fourteenth century, betraying, as they did, some advanced opinions for which the world at large was hardly then prepared.

Students of the manual, compendium, and popular handbook style of literature may possibly be hardly aware that the war of protection *versus* free trade, and the other war concerned with the incidence of taxation upon property, real and personal, had already begun. Even my distinguished friend, Mr. Cadaverous, who never made a mistake in his life, and whose memory for facts is portentous—even Mr. Cadaverous assures me that he has never met with any mention of the above fact in all his study of history.

History! What is history but the science which

teaches us to see the throbbing life of the present in the throbbing life of the past?

Note that these "gentlemen of the House of Commons," who made themselves somewhat dis-agreeable in the Parliament of 1348, were not the warriors who had gone out to fight the King's battles, but the burghers who stayed at home, heaped up money, and grumbled. It was otherwise with the roistering swash-bucklers who came back in that glorious autumn. They are said to have returned laden with the spoils of France, the plunder of Calais, and so on and so on. Calais must have been rather a queer little place to afford much *plunder* after all that it had gone through. The swash-bucklers doubtless brought prize-money home, but it did not all come from France—that is pretty certain. Villani, our Florentine friend, tells us of an unexampled commercial crisis at Florence about this time—brought about, observe, by the English conqueror of France not paying his debts. So the Bardi and the Peruzzi actually stopped payment; for the King owed them a million and a half of gold florins, and there was lamentation and distress of mind, and the level of the Arno rose by reason of the flood of tears that fell "from tired eyelids upon tired eyes." All that made no difference to the swash-bucklers, and up and down England there

was wild extravagance, and money seemed to burn
in people's pockets. Feasting and merriment, and
all that appertains thereto, were the order of the
day, and all went merry as a marriage bell.

The King got all he could get out of the Parliament, but he did not get, he could not get, all he
wished. What was to be done next? The Pope
said, " Make peace !" and his Holiness did his little
best to bring about the desired end. The summer
of 1348 had come, and it seems that at Avignon the
plague had by this time spent itself, people were
no longer afraid to go there now, and the Pope
would peradventure come out of his seclusion and
receive an embassy. So on the 28th of July Edward
III. wrote a letter to Pope Clement, and announced
his intention of sending his ambassadors to Avignon
to treat about terms. The negotiations fell through,
and on the 8th of October the King announced by
proclamation that he was once more going to make
an inroad upon France with an armed force. He
did not keep his word. In November a truce was
patched up somehow; and on the first of the next
month we find the King once more at Westminster,
and there he seems to have remained over Christmas.
If the dates are correctly given, the news from the
west of England about this time was not likely to
have provoked much merriment.

Are the dates correct? Gentlemen of an antiquarian turn of mind, out in the west there, might do worse than spend some weeks in looking into this matter.

Meanwhile, it is at this point that we get our first direct, unquestionable proof, that the plague had reached our shores. On the 1st of January, 1349, the King wrote to the Bishop of Winchester, informing him that although the Parliament had been summoned to meet on the 19th of the month, yet because a *sudden visitation of deadly pestilence had broken out at Westminster and the neighbourhood*, which was increasing daily, and occasioning much apprehension for the safety of any great concourse of people, should it assemble in that place at the time appointed; therefore it had been determined to prorogue the Parliament to Monday, the 27th of April.

I gather from the wording of this document that the Government did not look upon the outbreak with any very grave apprehension, that they did not regard it as anything more than an epidemic which would be confined to narrow limits, and one likely to pass off after a little time as the spring advanced; and that they can hardly as yet have received any very disturbing intelligence of its ravages, such as must have soon come in from all points of the compass. Two months passed, and the situation had seriously changed. On the 10th of March the King issued another letter, in which, after referring to the previous proclamation, he further prorogued the meeting of Parliament *sine die*. The reason for this step is explained to be "because the deadly pestilence in Westminster, *and in the City of London*, and in other places thereabouts, was increasing with extraordinary severity" (*gravius solito invalescit*).

It is to be observed that, in the first notice of prorogation, no mention is made of the City of London, only of Westminster and its neighbourhood. In the second, we hear that the plague had already extended over a wider area, and was showing no signs of abating. Nay, by this time the King and his advisers had taken alarm—there was no knowing where the mortality would stop.

Two days after this (12th of March, 1349) William Bateman, Bishop of Norwich, received his letters of protection as ambassador for the King in France. His safe conduct—for himself and his suite—was to extend till Whitsuntide next ensuing (31st of May, 1349). The suite consisted of eight persons, all Norfolk men; two were wealthy laymen, two were distinguished ecclesiastics, three were country parsons, of one I know nothing. I believe they all got back safely, but the three country parsons returned to their several cures only to be smitten by the plague. The Bishop had not shown himself again in his diocese many weeks before they were all three dead. In making this last statement, I am a little anticipating the course of events, but only a little. The Angel of Death moves at no laggard pace when once he begins his march with his sword drawn in his hand.

. . . . . .

Thus far I have been quoting from, or referring to, authorities which are accessible to any one with an adequate command of books at his elbow—the chroniclers and the historians named, the Fœdera, the Rolls of Parliament, and such authorities as whoever chooses may consult for himself. These printed authorities, which have all been consulted and looked into again and again, have told us very little, but they have given us certain notes of time— furnished us, in fact, with a *terminus a quo.* We have learnt this, at any rate, that about Christmas, 1348, the plague appeared at Westminster and its vicinity, and that it had increased alarmingly in London and elsewhere by the beginning of March, 1349.

We have next to deal with that other evidence to which I have alluded—the unprinted documentary evidence ready to our hands—I mean the Institution

Books in the various Diocesan Registries and the Rolls of the Manor Courts, which still exist in very great abundance, though they are rapidly disappearing from the face of the earth. It is necessary that I should trespass upon my reader's attention while I endeavour to explain the nature and the value of these two classes of documents before proceeding to deal with their testimony.

I. Students of English history know that few aggressions of the Pope of Rome during the thirteenth century caused more deep discontent among the laity than those which threatened interference with their right of patronage to ecclesiastical benefices, and actually did interfere with those rights. The disgraceful recklessness with which Italians, ignorant of our language, were forced into English livings, and the best preferment was claimed for Papal nominees, produced an amount of irritation and revolt against Roman interference which had never been known before. The feeling of the laity became more and more outspoken, and at last Innocent IV. gave way, and the rights of private patronage were assured to the great lords—assured, at any rate, in word—though the Papal rescript " paltered with them in a double sense," and the quibbles and reservations, which could always be resorted to under colour of the *non obstante* clause, constantly afforded excuse for fresh encroachments and evasions when the opportunity occurred. The jealousy of Roman interference continued to increase, and the legislation of the first half of the fourteenth century was largely taken up with enactments to guard the rights of English patrons, from the King downwards. But there was always a feeling of insecurity on the part of those who had any benefices in their gift, and a corresponding feeling on the part of those who were candidates for preferment. This led to a vicious system, whereby appointments were made with almost indecent haste to every vacant cure; institution was granted to an applicant for a benefice with the least possible delay after a vacancy had once been made known; the patron was willing to exercise his right in favour of any one, rather than not exercise it at all; the candidate for the living knew that it was a case of now or never; the Bishop had nothing to gain, and something to fear, from asking too many questions; and there is some reason to think that the parishioners had more voice in the matter than they have now. That followed which was likely to follow, namely, that the institutions to vacant benefices were made as a rule within a very few weeks, or even days, after the death of an incumbent. A man who had got his nomination lost no time in presenting himself to the Bishop. There

G

was no widow or family of his predecessor to consider; and for every reason, the sooner the new man got into the parsonage the better for all parties concerned. Moreover, to guard against all chances of a disputed claim, the Bishops' Registers of Institution were kept with the most scrupulous care, and while enormous masses of ecclesiastical records in every diocese in England have perished, the Institution Books have been preserved with extraordinary fidelity, have survived all the troubles and wars and spoliation that have gone on, and, speaking within certain limits, have been preserved for five hundred years from one end of England to the other. It is no exaggeration to say that there are hundreds of parishes in England of whose incumbents for centuries not only a complete list may be made out, but the very day and place be set down where those incumbents received institution into the benefice either at the hands of the Diocesan or his official. This is certainly the case in the great East Anglian diocese of Norwich, which comprehended, in the fourteenth century, the counties of Norfolk and Suffolk and a portion of Cambridgeshire. We may safely say that we are able to tell approximately—within a few weeks or days—when any living fell vacant during the period under review, who succeeded, and who the patron was who presented to the cure. Nor is this true only of the secular or parochial clergy. Jealous as the religious houses were of their rights and privileges, the heads of monasteries, as a rule, were compelled to receive institution too at the hands of the Bishops of the see in which they were situated. They too presented themselves to their Diocesan that their elections might be formally recognized; and thus the Institution Books contain not only the records of the various changes in the incumbency of the secular clergy, but also of such as were occasioned by the death of all abbots, or priors or abbesses as presided over that large number of religious houses as were not exempt from Episcopal jurisdiction. It is obvious that these Records constitute an invaluable body of evidence, from which important information may be drawn regarding our parochial and ecclesiastical history. The Institution Books, as might be expected, contain a great deal of curious matter besides the mere records of admission to benefices, but with this I am at present not concerned.

II. I come now to the Court Rolls, which throw much more light upon our parochial history than any other documents that have come down to us; their information is concerned exclusively with the civil, domestic, sometimes with the political life of our forefathers; about their religious life, or their contentions with ecclesiastics, they have rarely a word to say.

.　　　　　.　　　　　.

All who have at any time owned or purchased what is known as copyhold land might be supposed to know something of the nature of the title on which such land is held.　If they do not it is not for want of being reminded from time to time, in a very vexatious way, that they are in theory and in fact not so much owners of their several holdings as *tenants* of the Lord of the Manor to which such holdings appertain.　But inasmuch as a great deal of ignorance prevails as to the nature of this tenure, and as it is impossible to estimate the value and importance of the evidence which the Rolls of the Manor Courts supply in the inquiry on which we are engaged, I feel it necessary to introduce at this point a few paragraphs introductory to and explanatory of what follows.

.　　　.　　　.　　　.

In the thirteenth century it may be said that *in theory* the land of England belonged to the sovereign.

The sovereign had indeed assigned large tracts of territory to A or B or C; but under certain circumstances, of no very unfrequent occurrence, these tracts of territory came back into the hands of the sovereign, and were re-granted by him at his will to whom he chose. In return for such grants, A or B or C were bound to perform certain *services* in recognition of the fact that they were *tenants* of the king; and by virtue of such *services*—the equivalents of what we now understand by *rent*—they were called *tenants in chief*, or tenants *in capite*.

The tracts of territory held by A or B or C were in almost every case made up of lands scattered about over all parts of the kingdom. The tenant in chief had his castle or capital mansion,[1] which was supposed to be his abode; but as far as the larger portion—immensely the larger portion—of his possessions, he was necessarily a non-resident landlord, getting what he could out of them either by farming them through the agency of a bailiff, or letting out his estates to be held under himself in precisely the same way as he held his *fief*, or original grant, from the King.

In theory, the tenant in chief could not sell his

---

[1] Experts will object to the use of this term and other terms as strictly inaccurate. I am not writing for experts.

land; he could sublet it to a *mesne tenant*, who stood to himself precisely in the same relation as he—the tenant *in capite*—stood to the sovereign, the mesne tenant in his turn being bound to render certain *services* to his over lord, and liable to forfeit his *lease* —for in theory it was that—if certain contingencies happened. It was inevitable that, as time went by, the mesne tenant should regard his estate as his own, and that the same necessities which compelled the tenant *in capite* to relax his hold over an outlying landed estate would compel the mesne tenant to follow his example. The process went on till it was becoming a serious difficulty to discover how the King was to get his *services* from the tenant *in capite*, who had practically got rid of two-thirds of his *fief*, and how he again was to get *his services* from the mesne tenant, who had parted with two-thirds of *his* estate to half a dozen under tenants. Obviously, when the King's *scutage* had to be levied, there was no telling who was liable for it, or how it should be apportioned.

It was to meet this difficulty, and to check the prevailing sub-division of land—*sub-infeudation* men called it then—that the statute of *Quia Emptores* was passed in the eighteenth year of King Edward I. [A.D. 1290]. The result of all the sub-division that had been going on had been that the number of what we now call *landed estates* had largely increased, each of them administered on the model of the larger *fiefs* originally granted to the tenants *in capite.* There was a capital mansion in which the *lord* resided, or was supposed to reside, and sub-tenants holding their land under the lord, and paying to him periodically certain small money rents and rendering him certain *services.* The *estate* comprehended the capital mansion with its appurtenances and the domain lands in the lord's occupation, the common lands over which the tenants had certain common rights, and the lands in the occupation of the tenants, which they farmed with more or less freedom for their own behoof,—the whole constituting a manor whose owner was the lord. At certain intervals the tenants were bound to appear before their lord and give account of themselves ; bound, that is, to show cause why they had not performed their *services ;* bound to pay their quit rents, whether in money or kind ; bound to go through a great deal of queer business ; but above all, as far as our present purpose is concerned, *to do fealty* to the lord of the manor in every case where the small patches of land had changed hands, and pay a fine for entering upon land acquired by the various forms of alienation or by inheritance. In some manors, if a tenant died the lord laid claim to some of his live stock as a *heriot*, which was forthwith seized by the bailiff of the manor; and in all manors, if a man died without heirs, his land *escheated* to the lord of the manor; that is, it came back to the lord who *in theory* was the owner of the soil.

These periodical meetings at which all this business and a great deal else was transacted were called the *Courts* of the Manor, and the Records of these Courts were kept with exceeding and most jealous scrupulousness; they were invariably drawn up in Latin, according to a strictly legal form, and were inscribed on long *rolls* of parchment, and are known as Manor Court Rolls. This is not the time to say much more about the Court Rolls. They are not very easy reading—they require a somewhat long apprenticeship before they can be readily deciphered; but when one has once become familiar with them, they afford the student some very curious and unexpected information from time to time, though it must be allowed that you have to do a good deal of digging for every nugget that you find.

Observe, however, this—that it is not far from the truth to say that in East Anglia—for I will not travel out of my own province—every tiller of the soil who occupied a plot of land, however small, was sure to be a tenant under some lord of the manor; when he died *a record of his death was entered upon the*

Court Rolls of the Manor; the name of his successor was inscribed; the amount of fine set down which his heir paid for entering upon his inheritance; and if he died *without heirs* the fact was noticed, the lands which he had held being forfeited, or *escheating*, as it was called, to the lord.

Thus the Court Rolls of a manor of the fourteenth century—for before the statute *Quia Emptores* I suspect that they were kept with much less regularity and much less care than they were afterwards—are practically the *registers of the deaths* of all occupiers of land within the manor; and, as every householder was an occupier of land, the death of every householder may be said to be inscribed upon the Rolls.

    .   .   .   .   .

Taken together, then, we have in the Diocesan Institution Books, on the one hand, and in the Court Rolls, on the other, two sources of information which—as far as they go—furnish us with a mass of evidence absolutely irrefragable with regard to the mortality of clergy and laity at any period during the fourteenth century. I say "as far as they go," for it might happen that a country benefice—and still more frequently that a town benefice—had been so cruelly pillaged by a religious house, that little or nothing remained to support the wretched parson, and that no one could be found who would accept the cure. Then the cure would remain vacant for years. Where this happened the death of the previous incumbent would not appear on the Records for years after it had occurred, nor would any notice be taken of the long vacancy when the next parson was instituted. In a period of dreadful mortality, if the parsons died off in large numbers, it would be inevitable that the impoverished livings would " go a begging." It might be difficult to get the most valuable pieces of preferment filled—it would be impossible to fill such as could not offer a bare maintenance. Hence the Institution Books can only be accepted as giving a part of the evidence with regard to the clerical mortality. However startling the number of deaths of clergy within a certain area during a given period may appear to be, they certainly will not represent the whole number—only the number of such incumbents as were forthwith replaced by their successors ; and, taking one year with another, it is fair to say that within any diocese the *larger the number of institutions* recorded in a given time, the *more incomplete* will be the record of the deaths among the clergy during that time. When there are more men than places the places are soon filled. When there are more places than men there must needs be vacancies—square holes and round ones.

So much for the Institution Books. With regard to the Court Rolls, there the evidence is even much less exhaustive; for here we have the registers of the deaths of the landholders within the manor, great and small—*i.e.*, of the heads of families; but, except in rare instances, we have no notice of any other member of the household, or of what happened to them. A man's whole household may have been swept off—young and old, babe and suckling, sister and brother, and aged mother, and wife, and children, and servant, and friend—every soul of them involved in one hideous, horrible calamity. The steward of the manor was not concerned with any but the head of the house—the tenant of the manor. Was he missing? Then, who was his heir? Any sons? Dead of the plague! Brothers? Dead of the plague! Wife? Dead of the plague! Children? Kinsfolk? All gone! Their blackening carcases huddled in sweltering masses of putrefaction in the wretched hovels, while the pitiless July sun blazed overhead, "Calmer than clock-work, and not caring!"

The steward made his entry of one fact only. Thus :—

"The Jurors do present that Simon Must died seized of a Messuage and 4 acres of land in Stradset, and that he has no heir. Therefore it is fitting

that the aforesaid land be taken into the hands of
the lord."

Also that Matilda Stile . . . was she married or
single, widow or mother or maid ? What cared the
precise man of business on that 24th of July, 1349,
as his pen moved over the parchment ? . . .—" Matilda Stile died seized of one acre and one rood of
land held in Villenage. Therefore it is fitting that
the aforesaid land be taken into the hands of the
lord until such time as the heir may appear in court."

He never did appear ! Next year her little estate
was handed over to another. She was the last of
her line.

Such entries as these swarm in the Court Rolls of
this year 1349. They tell their own tale. But it
is obvious that their tale is incomplete, and that we
must form our own conclusions from the number of
the deaths recorded as to the probable number of
those whose names have been quite passed over.
sometimes, too, these Rolls are eloquent in their
silence. When country parsons were dying by
scores and hundreds, and the tillers of the soil by
thousands and tens of thousands, it could not but be
that the lords of manors and their stewards died
also. Yes ! they, too, were struck down. In one
instance that I have met with the first half of the
entries of the business carried on at one of these

courts in the summer of this year is written in the ordinary court hand of the time, and the rest is rudely scrawled by some one whose hand *is not yet formed;* it looks like the writing of a lad apprenticed to the scrivener's business. Was the steward of the manor actually smitten by the plague as he was holding the court—a subordinate taking his place and awkwardly finishing the work which his master's glazed eye perhaps never rested on? Again and again I have found that a series of Court Rolls of an important Norfolk manor is perfect for the first twenty-two years of Edward III. and no record remains for the next year or two. Then they begin once more, and have been preserved with unbroken regularity. At Raynham, in a parish of 1,400 acres, there were three small manors. The courts of one of them were held three times in the year 1348. *Upon the same parchment,* and immediately following the records of the previous year, come some scarcely legible notes of a court held in 1349, the precise day of the month omitted, the entries scrawled informally by a scribe who not only did not know the forms of the court, but who was evidently not a professional writer. He bungled so that he seems actually to have given up his task. The next court of the manor was not held till three years had gone by. At Hellhoughton, a manor now belonging to the

Marquis of Townshend, where two courts were held annually, the series of rolls for the first twenty-two years of Edward III. is complete. Then comes one which scarcely deserves to be called a Court Roll, so entirely informal is it, and so evidently drawn up by some one who did not know his business, and who did not pretend to know it. It is little more than a collection of rough memoranda of deaths. Twelve of the *suitors* of the court had died without heirs; seven others had come to do fealty to the lord as successors to those whose heirs they presumably were. Nothing else is recorded. At another manor of Lord Townshend's, Raynham Parva, between the years 1347 and 1350 no court seems to have been held, though the lord of the manor, Thomas de Ingaldesthorp, had died in the interval. The scourge of the plague had been so awful in its incidence that when the next court was held on the 24th July, 1350, fourteen men and four women (holders of land, be it remembered) are named as having died off, not one of whom had left a living representative behind them. In all cases their little holdings had escheated to the lord. Amongst them was one " John Taleour, clericus." Was he the clerk who, up to this time, had kept the Rolls so neatly, and who could not be easily replaced after he fell a victim to the plague ?

Indeed, the inquirer who is desirous of pursuing researches in this field must be prepared for frequent disappointment just at the moment when he thinks he has made a "find." The Court Rolls for this particular year are comparatively scarce, and this is true not only for East Anglia, but for the whole of England, as any one may see who will only cast his eye down those pages of the Deputy-Keeper's Forty-third Annual Report, which are concerned with the Records of the Duchy of Lancaster. These *registers of deaths* are, as I have before said, only *complete as far as they go.*

. . . . . .

Let us now return to the point at which the King's letter of prorogation left us on the 10th March, 1349. At that time it is certain that the pestilence was raging fiercely in London and Westminster, and almost as certain that it had abated in Avignon and other towns in France. Two or three days after this date the Bishop of Norwich crossed the Channel, leaving his diocese in the hands of his officials. Had the plague broken out with any severity in East Anglia? I think it almost demonstrable that it had not. A day or two before the Bishop left London he instituted his friend Stephen de Cressingham to the Deanery of Cranwich—in the west of Norfolk—which had fallen vacant, but there is nothing to show that the vacancy was due to anything out of the common. During the year ending 25th of March, 1349, there were 80 institutions in the diocese of Norwich, as against 92 in the year 1347 and 59 in the year 1346. The average number of institutions for the five years ending 25th of March, 1349, was 77. Between this date and the end of the month there were four institutions only—that is, there was nothing abnormal in the condition of the diocese.

East Anglia had not long to wait. In the valley of the Stour, a mile or two from Sudbury, where the stream serves as the boundary between Suffolk and Essex, the ancestors of Lord Walsingham had two manors in the township of Little Cornard—the one was called Caxtons, the other was the Manor of Cornard Parva. At this latter manor a court was held on the 31st of March—the number of tenants of the manor can at no time have exceeded fifty— yet at this court six women and three men are registered as having died since the last court was held, two months before.

This is the earliest instance I have yet met with of the appearance of the plague among us, and as it is the earliest, so does it appear to have been one of the most frightful visitations from which any town or village in Suffolk or Norfolk suffered during the time the pestilence lasted. On the 1st of May another court was held, fifteen more deaths are recorded—thirteen men and two women. *Seven of them without heirs.* On the 3rd of November, apparently when the panic abated, again the court met. In the six months that had passed thirty-six more deaths had occurred, and *thirteen more households* had been left without a living soul to represent them. In this little community, in six months' time, twenty-one families had been absolutely obliterated — men, women and children—and of the rest it is difficult to see how there can have been a single house in which there was not one dead. Meanwhile, some time in September, the parson of the parish had fallen a victim to the scourge, and on the 2nd of October another was instituted in his room. Who reaped the harvest? The tithe sheaf too — how was it garnered in the barn? And the poor kine at milking time? Hush! Let us pass on.

. . . . . .

Little Cornard lies almost at the extreme south of the county of Suffolk. At the extreme north of Norfolk, occupying the elbow of the coast, having the Wash on the west and the German Ocean on the north, lies the deanery of Heacham, a district in which the Le Stranges have for at least seven centuries exercised their beneficent influence. Heacham itself is a large township extending over some 4,900 acres. The manorial rights appear to have extended over the whole parish. The series of Court Rolls is almost unbroken for the reign of Edward III. During the years 1346, 1347, and 1348, ten, six, and nine deaths are registered respectively. The courts were held every two months. In December, 1348, there is no death recorded; in February, 1349, again there is none. On the 28th of April a dispute was set down for hearing to be adjudicated upon by the steward and a jury of the homage. It was a dispute between a husband and wife on a question of dower. The man's name was Reginald Goscelin, his wife's name was Emma. The dispute was never settled. Before the day of hearing came on, *every one* of Emma Goscelin's witnesses was dead, and her husband was dead too. Four other landowners had died. One of these latter had a son and heir to succeed, but two months later the boy had gone, and the sole representative of the family was a little girl, who became straightway the ward of the lord of the manor.

Contiguous to the township of Heacham lies Hunstanton—not the pleasant little watering-place which the million will persist in calling by that name, though scarcely forty years ago the maker and builder of the modern town, the man who marked out its streets and planned its roads, and foresaw its future before a brick of the place was laid, gave it the name of St. Edmunds—Hunstanton, I say, in the fourteenth century was a parish less than half the size of Heacham, and probably much further from the sea than it is now. When, on the 20th of March, 1349, the steward of the manor of Hunstanton held his court there he entered the name of only one old woman who had died within the last month—that is, up to the 20th of March the plague had not yet appeared. Five weeks after this, on the 23rd of April, the next court was held. Five petty disputes had been entered for hearing. Sixteen men were engaged in them as principals or witnesses. When the day came eleven of the sixteen were dead. On the 22nd of May again there was a court, and again three suits for debt were set down. The defendant in one case, the plaintiff in a second, both plaintiff and defendant in the third, died before the court day arrived. In June no court was held—was there a panic? Except in this month and in September the meetings were carried on as regularly as if it had all been done by machinery. In September things got to their worst, and in this month the parson died, and was speedily succeeded by another. When the court of the 16th of October sat, it was found that in two months sixty-three men and fifteen women had been carried off.   In thirty-one instances there were only women or children to succeed; in nine cases there were no heirs, and the little estates had escheated to the lord.   Incredible though it may sound the fact is demonstrable, that in this one parish of Hunstanton, which a man may walk round in two or three hours, and the whole population of which might have assembled in the church then recently built, one hundred and seventy-two persons, tenants of the manor, died off in eight months; seventy-four of them left no heirs male, and nineteen others had no blood relation in the world to claim the inheritance of the dead.

I have no intention of laying before my readers a detailed statement of the documentary evidence which has passed under my notice.   The time has not come yet for an elaborate report on the case, nor can I pretend to have done more than break ground upon what must be regarded still as virgin soil; but this I may safely say, that I have not found one single roll of any Norfolk manor during this dreadful 23rd year of Edward, dating after April or May, which did not contain only too abundant proof of the ravages of the pestilence—evidence which forces upon me the conviction that hardly a town or village in East Anglia escaped the scourge; and which in its cumulative force makes it impossible to doubt that the mortality in Norfolk and Suffolk must have exceeded the largest estimate which has yet been given by conjecture.

When I find in a stray roll of an insignificant little manor at Croxton, near Thetford, held on the 24th of July, that seventeen tenants had died since the last court, eight of them without heirs; that at another court held the *same day* at Raynham, at the other end of the county, eighteen tenements had fallen into the lord's hands, eight of them certainly escheated, and the rest retained *until the appearance of the heir;* that in the manor of Hadeston, a hamlet of Bunwell, twelve miles from Norwich, which could not possibly have had four hundred inhabitants, fifty-four men and fourteen women were carried off by the pestilence in six months, twenty-four of them without a living soul to inherit their property; that in manor after manor the lord was carried off as well as the tenants and the steward; that in a single year *upwards of eight hundred parishes lost their parsons,* eighty-three of them twice, and ten of them three times in a few months; and that it is quite certain these large numbers represent only a portion of the mortality among the clergy and the religious orders—when, I say, I consider all this and a great deal more that might be dwelt on, I see no other conclusion to arrive at but one, namely, that during the year ending March, 1350, more than half the population of East Anglia was swept away by the Black Death. If any one should suggest that *many more* than half died, I should not be disposed to quarrel with him.

It must be remembered that nothing has been here said of the mortality in the towns. I believe we have no means of getting at any evidence on this part of the subject which can be trusted. In no part of England did the towns occupy a more important position relatively to the rest of the population. In no part of England did three such important towns as Lynn, Yarmouth, and Norwich, lie within so short a distance of one another, not to mention others which were then rising in the number and consideration of their inhabitants. But the statements made of the mortality in the towns will not bear examination—they represent mere guesses, nothing more. This, however, may be assumed as certain— that the death-rate in the towns at such a time as this cannot have been *less* than the death-rate in the villages, and that the scourge which so cruelly devastated the huts and cabins of the countrymen was not likely to fall less heavily upon the filthy dens and hovels of the men of the streets. Town life in the fourteenth century was a very dreadful life for the masses.

How did the great bulk of the people comport themselves under the pressure of this unparalleled calamity? How did their faith stand the strain that was put upon it? How did their moral instincts support them? Was there any confusion and despair? What effects—social, political, economical—followed from a catastrophe so terrible? How did the clergy behave during the tremendous ordeal through which they had to pass? What glimpses do we get of the horrors or the sorrows of that time—of the romantic, of the pathetic side of life?

V.

THE BLACK DEATH IN EAST ANGLIA.

(CONTINUED.)

WHEN Bishop Bateman started on his journey upon the King's business, in March 1349, he can scarcely have turned his back upon his diocese without some misgivings as to what might happen during his absence. In some parts of Norfolk a very grievous murrain had prevailed during the previous year among the live stock in the farms, and though this had almost disappeared, there was ample room for anxiety in the outlook. If the plague had not yet been felt to any extent in East Anglia, it might burst forth any day. London had been stricken already, and there was no saying where it would next appear in its most malignant form. It was hoped that the Bishop's mission would be accomplished in a couple of months, and during his absence the charge of the diocese was committed as usual to his officials, to one of whom the palace at Norwich was assigned as a temporary residence.

The good ship, with the Bishop and his suite, had hardly got out of the channel, when a storm other than that which sailors care for burst upon town and village in East Anglia. The Bishop's official found his hands full of work. In April he was called upon to institute twenty-three parsons to livings that had fallen vacant. This was bad enough as a beginning, but it was child's play to what followed. By the end of May *seventy-four* more cures had lost their incumbents and been supplied with successors. That is, in a single month, the number of institutions throughout the diocese had almost equalled the *annual* average of the last five years. All these stricken parishes were country villages, and the larger number of them lay to the north and east of the county of Norfolk. We take note of this that we call a fact, and straightway the temptation presents itself to construct a theory upon it. Who knows not that in the trying spring-time, the " colic of puff'd Aquilon " makes life hard for man and beast in Norfolk, and that across our fields the cruel gusts burst upon us with a bitter petulance, unsparing, pitiless, hateful, till our vitality seems to be steadily waning? It was in the month of March that the great plague smote us first :—did it not come to us on the wings of the wind that swept across the sea the germs of pestilence, say from Norway, or some neighbour land in which, peradventure, the Black Death had already spent itself in hideous havoc? A tempting theory! If I confess that such a view once presented itself to my own mind I am compelled to acknowledge that I abandoned it with reluctance. It was hard, but it had to be done. How we all do hanker after a theory! What! live all your life without a theory? It's as dreary a prospect as living all your life without a baby, and yet some few great men have managed to pass through life placidly without the one or the other, and have not died forgotten or lived forlorn.

The plague had apparently fallen with the greatest virulence upon the coast and along the watercourses, but already in the spring had reached the neighbourhood of Norwich, and was showing an unsparing impartiality in its visitation. At Earlham and Wytton and Horsford, at Taverham and Bramerton, all of them villages within five miles of the cathedral, the parsons had already died. Round the great city, then the second city in England, village was being linked to village closer and closer every day in one ghastly chain of death. What a ring-fence of horror and contagion for all comers and goers to overpass!

For two months Thomas de Methwold, the official, stayed where he had been bidden to stay, in the thick of it all, at the palace. On the 29th of May he could bear it no longer. Do you ask was he afraid? Not so! We shall see that he was no craven; but the bravest men are not reckless, and least of all are they the men who are careless about the lives or the feelings of others. The great cemetery of the city of Norwich was at this time actually within the cathedral Close. The whole of the large space enclosed between the nave of the cathedral on the south and the bishop's palace on the east, and stretching as far as the Erpingham gate on the west, was one huge graveyard. When the country parsons came to present themselves for institution at the palace, they had to pass straight across this cemetery. The tiny churchyards of the city, demonstrably very little if at all larger than they are now, were soon choked, the soil rising higher and higher above the level of the street, which even to this day is in some cases five or six feet below the soppy sod piled up within the old enclosures. To the great cemetery within the Close the people brought their dead, the tumbrels discharging their load of corpses all day long, tilting

them into the huge pits made ready to receive them;
the stench of putrefaction palpitating through the
air, and borne by the gusts of the western breeze
through the windows of the palace, where the
Bishop's official sat, as the candidates knelt before
him and received institution with the usual formali-
ties.   It was hard upon him, it was doubly so upon
those who had travelled a long day's journey through
the pestilential villages; and on the 30th of May the
official removed from Norwich to Terlyng, in Essex,
where the Bishop had a residence; there he remained
for the next ten days, during which time he instituted thirty-nine more parsons to their several
benefices.   By this time other towns in the
diocese had felt the force of the visitation.   Ipswich
had been smitten, and Stowmarket, and East Dereham—how many more we cannot tell.   Then the
news came that the Bishop had returned; Thomas
de Methwold was at once ordered back to Norwich—
come what might, that was his post; there he should
stay, whether to live or die.

The Bishop seems to have landed at Yarmouth
about the 10th of June; he did not at once push on
to report himself to the King; urgent private affairs
detained him in his native county.   Seventeen or
eighteen miles to the south-west of Yarmouth lies
the village of Gillingham, where the Bishop's

brother, Sir Bartholomew Bateman, a man of great wealth and consideration, had been the lord of the manor. The parish contains about 2,000 acres, and at this time had at least three churches, only one of which now remains. Besides these Sir Bartholomew had a private chapel in his house. Here he kept up much state, as befitted a personage who had more than once represented Norfolk and Suffolk in Parliament. The plague came, and the worthy knight was struck down; the parson too fell a victim; and the Lady Petronilla, Sir Bartholomew's widow, presented to the living a certain Hugh Atte Mill, who was instituted on the 7th of June. The first news that the Bishop heard when he landed was that his brother was dead. He started off at once to Gillingham. Death had been busy all around, and the plague had broken out in the Benedictine Nunnery of Bungay and carried off the prioress among others. Straightway the few nuns that were left chose another prioress; on the morning of the 13th she came for institution, and received it at the Bishop's hands. Hurrying on to Norwich, the Bishop stayed but a single day, leaving his official at the palace. He himself had to present himself before the King to give account of his mission; on the 19th he was in London; on the 4th of July he was back again in his diocese. During the twenty days that had passed since he had left Gillingham, exactly *one hundred* clergymen had been admitted to vacant cures, all of them crossing the horrible cemetery where the callous gravediggers were at work night and day, the sultry air charged with suffocating stench, poisoning the breath of heaven. Yet there the Bishop's vicar-general had to stay, eat, drink, and sleep—if he could—and there he did stay till the Bishop came back and relieved him of the dreadful work.

Meanwhile the gentry too had been dying. It is clear that in the upper ranks the men died more frequently than the women, explain it how you will. During June and July no fewer than fifteen patrons of livings were widows, while in thirteen other benefices the patronage was in the hands of the executors or trustees of gentlemen who had died. During the month of July in scarcely a village within five miles of Norwich had the parson escaped the mortality, yet in Norwich the intrepid Bishop remained in the very thick of it all, as if he would defy the angel of death, or at least show an example of the loftiest courage. Only towards the end of July did he yield, perhaps, to the persuasion or entreaty of others, and moved away to the southern part of his diocese, taking up his residence at Hoxne, in Suffolk, where he stayed till October, when he once more returned to his house at Thorpe by Norwich. The palace had become at last absolutely uninhabitable.

To Hoxne accordingly the newly-appointed clergy came in troops, and during the first seven weeks after the Bishop's arrival he admitted no less than eighty-two parsons, a larger number than had been the average of a whole year heretofore. Did they all betake themselves to their several parishes and brave the peril and set themselves to the grim work before them? They could not help themselves. Where the benefice was a vicarage an oath to reside upon his cure was in every case rigorously imposed upon the newly-appointed; and though the law did not sanction this in the case of rectors, yet not a single instance of a licence of non-residence occurs; the difficulty of finding substitutes was becoming daily more and more insuperable, and the penalty of deserting a parish without licence was a great deal too serious to be disregarded. In the months of June, July, and August things were at their worst, as might have been expected. In July alone there were two hundred and nine institutions. During the year ending March, 1350, considerably more than two-thirds of the benefices of the diocese had become vacant.

In the religious houses the plague wrought, if

possible, worse havoc still. There were seven nunneries in Norfolk and Suffolk. Five of them lost their prioresses. How many poor nuns were taken who can guess? In the College of St. Mary-in-the-fields, at Norwich, five of the seven prebendaries died. In September the abbot of St. Benet's Hulm was carried off. Again we ask and receive no answer—what must have been the mortality among the monks and the servants of the convent? And yet sometimes we do get an answer to that question. In the house of Augustinian Canons at Heveringland prior and canons died to a man. At Hickling, which a century before had been a flourishing house and been doing good work, only one canon survived. Neither of these houses ever recovered from the effects of the visitation; they were eventually absorbed in other monastic establishments.

It is one of the consequences of the peculiar privileges granted to the Friars that no notice of them occurs in the episcopal records. They were free lances with whom the bishops had little to do. It is only by the accident of every one of the Friars of our Lady who had a house in Norwich having been carried off, and the fact that their house was left tenantless, that we know anything of their fate. Wadding, the great annalist of the Franciscans, while deploring the notorious decadence in the *morale* of the mendicant orders during the fourteenth century—a decadence which he does not attempt to deny—attributes it wholly to the action of the Black Death, and is glad to find in that calamity a sufficient cause for accounting for the loss of the old prestige which in little more than a century after St. Francis's death had set in so decidedly. "It was from this cause," he writes, "that the monastic bodies, and especially the mendicant orders, which up to this time had been flourishing in virtue and learning, began to decline, and discipline to become slack; as well from the loss of eminent men as from the relaxation of the rules, in consequence of the pitiable calamities of the time; and it was vain to look for reform among the young men and the promiscuous multitude who were received without the necessary discrimination, for they thought more of filling the empty houses than of restoring the old strictness that had passed away."

How could it be otherwise? In the two counties of Norfolk and Suffolk, at least *nineteen* religious houses were left without prior or abbot. We may be quite sure that where the chief ruler dropped off the brethren of the house and the army of servants and hangers-on did not escape. What happened at the great Abbey of St. Edmund's we know not yet, and until we get more light it is idle to conjecture but, as a man stands in that vast graveyard at Bury,

H

and looks around him, he can hardly help trying—trying, but failing—to imagine what the place must have looked like when the plague was raging. What a Valley of Hinnom it must have been! Those three mighty churches, all within a stone's throw of one another, and one of them just one hundred feet longer than the cathedral at Norwich, sumptuous with costly offerings, and miracles of splendour within—and outside ghastly heaps of corruption, and piles of corpses waiting their turn to be covered up with an inch or two of earth. Who can adequately realize the horrors of that awful summer? In the desolate swamps through which the sluggish Bure crawls reluctantly to mingle its waters with the Yare; by the banks of the Waveney where the little Bungay nunnery had been a refuge for the widow, the forsaken, or the devout for centuries; in the valley of the Nar—the Norfolk Holy Land—where seven monasteries of one sort or another clustered, each distant from the other but a few short miles—among the ooze and sedge and chill loneliness of the Broads, where the tall reeds wave and whisper, and all else is silent—the glorious buildings with their sumptuous churches were little better than centres of contagion. From the stricken towns people fled to the monasteries, lying away there in their seclusion, safely, favoured of God. If there was hope anywhere it must be there. As frightened widows and orphans flocked to these havens of refuge, they carried the Black Death with them, and when they dropped death-stricken at the doors, they left the contagion behind them as their only legacy. Guilty wretches with a load of crime upon their consciences—desperate as far as this world was concerned, and ready for any act of wickedness should the occasion arrive—shuddered lest they should go down to burning flame for ever now that there was none to shrive them or to give the *viaticum* to any late penitent in his agony. In the tall towers by the wayside the bells hung mute ; no hands to ring them or none to answer to their call· Meanwhile, across the lonely fields, toiling dismally, and ofttimes missing the track—for who should guide them or show the path ?—parson and monk and trembling nun made the best of their way to Norwich ; their errand to seek admission to the vacant preferment. Think of them, after miles of dreary travelling, reaching the city gates at last, and shudderingly threading the filthy alleys which then served as streets, stepping back into doorways to give the dead carts passage, and jostled by lepers and outcasts, the touch of whose garments was itself a horror. Think of them staggering across the great cemetery and stumbling over the rotting carcases not yet committed to the earth, breathing all the while the tainted breath of corruption—sickening, loathsome! Think of them returning as they came, going over the same ground as before, and compelled to gaze again at

> Sights that haunt the soul for ever,
> Poisoning life till life is done.

Think of them foot-sore, half-famished, hardly daring to buy bread and meat for their hunger, or to beg a cup of cold water for Christ's sake, or entreat shelter for the night in their faintness and weariness, lest men should cry out at them—"Look! the Black Death has clutched another of the doomed!"

.   .   .   .   .   .

I have said that upwards of 800 of the beneficed clergy perished in East Anglia during this memorable year. Besides these we must make allowance for the non-beneficed among the regulars; the *chaplains*, who were in the position of curates among ourselves; the vicars of parishes whose endowments were insufficient to maintain a resident parson under ordinary circumstances, and the members of the monastic and mendicant orders. Putting all these together, it seems to me that we cannot estimate the number of deaths among regular and secular clergy in East Anglia during the year 1349 at less than *two thousand.*[1] This may appear an enormous number at first hearing, but it is no incredible number. Unfortunately the earliest record of any ordinations in the diocese of Norwich dates nearly seventy years after the plague year, but there is every reason for believing that there were at least *as many*, and probably many more, candidates at ordinations in the fourteenth century as presented themselves in the fifteenth. During the year ending January, 1415, Bishop Courtenay's suffragan ordained 382 persons, and assuming that in Bishop Bateman's days an equal number were admitted to the clerical profession, the losses by death in the plague year would have absorbed all the clergy who had been ordained during the six previous years, but no more. Even so this constituted a tremendous strain upon the reserve force of clergy unbeneficed and more or less unemployed, and it was inevitable that with such a strain, there would be a deterioration in the character and fitness of the newly-appointed incumbents. Yet nothing has surprised me more than the exceeding rareness of evidence damaging to the reputation of the

[1] In the diocese of Ely, where the mortality was less severe than in Norfolk and Suffolk, 57 parsons died in the three months ending the 1st of October, 1349. When an ordination was held by the Bishop of Ely's suffragan at the priory of Barnwell on the 19th of September, the newly-ordained were fewer by 35 than those who had died at their posts since the last ordination.

new men. That these men were less educated than
their predecessors we know; but that they were
mere worthless hypocrites there is nothing to show,
and much to disprove. Nay! the strong impression
which has been left upon my mind, and which gathers
strength as I study the subject, is that the parochial
clergy of the fourteenth century, before *and after* the
plague, were decidedly a better set than the clergy of
the thirteenth. The friars had done some of their
best work in " provoking to jealousy " the country
clergy and stimulating them to increased faithful-
ness ; they had, in fact, made them more *respectable* ;
just as the Wesleyan revival acted upon the country
parsons and others four centuries later. Until the
episcopal *visitations* of the monasteries during the
fourteenth and fifteenth centuries are made public—
they exist in far larger numbers than is usually supposed—it will be impossible to estimate the effect of
the plague upon the religious houses ; but I am inclined to think that the monasteries suffered very
greatly indeed from the terrible visitation, and that
the violent disturbance of the old traditions and the
utter breakdown in the old observances acted as
disastrously upon these institutions as the first stroke
of paralysis does upon men who have passed their
prime—they never were again what they had been.

It must be remembered that in the great majority

of the smaller monasteries, and indeed in any religious house where there were chaplains to do the routine work in the church, there was nothing to prevent an absolutely illiterate man or woman from becoming monk or nun. It was, however, impossible for a man to discharge the duties of his calling as a parish priest without some education and without at least a knowledge of Latin. I will not stop to argue that point ; they who dispute the assumption have much to learn. Moreover it is only what we should expect, that while some were hardened and brutalized by the scenes through which they had passed, some were softened and humbled. The prodigious activity in church building — church *restoration* is perhaps the truer term—during the latter part of the fourteenth century in East Anglia is one of many indications that the religious life of the people at large had received a mighty stimulus. Here, again, the evidence near at hand requires to be carefully looked into. In historical no less than in physical researches, the microscope requires to be used. As yet it has scarcely been used at all. History is in the empirical stage. Meanwhile, such hints as that of Knighton's are significant when he tells us that, as the parsons died, a vast multitude of laymen whose wives had perished in the pestilence presented themselves for holy orders. *Many*, he

says—not all—were illiterate, save that they knew
how to read their missals and go through the services
though unintelligently, they hardly understood what
they read. Were they, therefore, the worst of the
new parsons ? Men bowed down by a great sorrow,
bewildered by a bereavement for which there is
none but a make-shift remedy, men whose "life is
read all backwards and the charm of life undone,"
are not they whose sorrow usually makes them void
of sympathy for the distressed. Nay ! their own
sadness makes them responsive to the cry of the
needy, the lonely, and the fallen. Experience proves
to us every day that among such men you may find,
not the worst parish priests, but the best.

. . . . . .

I wonder whether John Bonington, steward of
the manor of Waltham, was one of those whom
Knighton alludes to.

Sometime during the year 1343 there had been a
disastrous fire in the house of one Roger Andrew;
the dwelling, with all that it contained, was burnt
to the ground. Poor Roger lost all his household
stuff and furniture and much else besides; worse
than all, he lost all his title deeds, the evidences and
charters whereby he held his little estate. As for
Roger himself, he either perished in the flames or
his heart broke and he died very shortly afterwards.

He left a son behind him, young Richard Andrew, who must have found himself in sorry plight when he came to take up his patrimony and enter upon his inheritance. Those were not the days when the weak man and the beaten man excited much pity in England. No! they were *not*, whatever sentimental people may say who maunder about the ages of faith and refresh themselves with other such lackadaisical phrases. So, poor Richard being down in his luck, John Bonington, acting for Henry, Earl of Lancaster,[1] the lord of the manor, put the screw on, and boldly claimed a heriot from the young man as the right of the lord. Richard disputed the right, and protested that his land was not *heriotable*. Bonington pleaded his *might* in a very effectual way, and took his heriot —to wit, the best horse which Richard had in his stable, the best and probably the only one. Then Richard appealed to the homage. The homagers were afraid to give a verdict against the steward, and timidly objected that all Richard's evidences had been burnt in the fire. Bonington trotted off triumphant, leaving Richard to his bitter wrath. Six years went by, and the plague came. It fell upon the district round with terrific fury, and the people died in that dreadful April, 1349, as the locusts die when the hurricane drives them seaward, and they rot in piles upon the shore. The Roll of

[1] His son and heir, Henry, Earl of Derby, was created *Duke* of Lancaster in 1351.

H 2

the Manor Court is a horrible record of the suddenness and the force with which the Black Death smote the wretched Essex people. When the steward's day's work was done, and the long, long list of the dead had been written down, he added a note wherein he gives us the facts which have come down to us; and then he adds that, inasmuch as he, John Bonington, had come to see that the aforesaid horse had been unrighteously taken from Richard Andrew six years before, and that the conviction of his own iniquity had been brought home to his contrite heart, *as well by the dreadful mortality and horrible pestilence at that time raging as by the stirring of religious emotion within his soul*, therefore the full value of the horse was to be restored to the injured Richard, and never again was heriot to be levied on his land. After six years' hard riding and scant feeding, peradventure Richard Andrew would rather have had the hard cash than the poor brute, which by this time, probably, had died and gone to the dogs! A shudder of penitence and remorse had thrilled through John Bonington when the plague was stalking grimly up and down the land; and this is what we learn about him—this and no more.

Had John Bonington lost *his* wife; and was he meditating a life of usefulness and penitence and prayer?

Infert se sæptus nebula (mirabile dictu)
Per medios miscetque viris, neque cernitur ulli.

A shadowy form looming out from the mists that
have gathered over the ages past, we see him for a
moment, and he is gone.

Fill up the gaps and tell all the tale, poet with the
dreamy eyes, eyes that can pierce the gloom—poet
with the mobile lips, lips that can speak with rhyth-
mic utterance the revelations of the future or the
past.

All the lonely ones, and all the childless ones, did
not turn parsons we may be sure; yet it is good for
us to believe that John Bonington's was not a
solitary instance of a man coming out of the furnace
of affliction softened, not hardened; purified, not
merely blistered, by the fire.

Was Thomas Porter at Little Cornard somewhat
past his prime when the plague came? It spared
him and his old wife, it seems; but for his sons and
daughters, the hope of his eld and the pride of his
manhood, where were they? He and the good wife,
cowering over the turf fire, did they dare to talk
with quivering lips and clouded eyes about the days
when the little ones had clambered up to the strong
father's knee, or tiny arms were held out to the
rough yeoman as he reached his home? "Oh! the
desolation and the loneliness. No fault of thine,

dear wife—nor mine. It is the Lord, let Him do
what seemeth Him good!"

Thomas Porter had a neighbour, one John Stone,
a man of small substance: he owned a couple of
acres under the lord; poor land it was, hardly
paying for the tillage, and I suppose the cottage
upon it was his own, so far as any man's copyhold
dwelling was his own in those days. The Black
Death came to that cottage among the rest, and
John Stone and wife and children, all were swept
away. Nay! not all: little Margery Stone was
spared; but she had not a kinsman upon earth.
Poor little maid, she was barely nine years old and
absolutely alone! Who cared? Thomas Porter
and his weeping wife cared, and they took little
Margery to their home, and they comforted themselves for all that they had lost, and the little maid
became unto them as a daughter. Henceforth life
was less dreary for the old couple. But five years
passed, and Margery had grown up to be a sturdy
damsel and very near the marriageable age.

Oh, ho! friend Porter, what is it we have heard
men tell? That when the Black Death came upon
us, your house was left unto you desolate and there
remained neither chick nor child. Who is this?
Then some one told the steward, or told the lord,
and thereupon ensued inquiry. What right had

Thomas Porter to adopt the child? She belonged to the lord, and he had the right of guardianship. Aye! and the right of disposing of her in marriage too. Thomas Porter, with a heavy heart, was summoned before the homage. He pleaded that the marriage of the girl did not belong to the lord by right, and that on some ground or other, which is not set down, she was not his property at all. That might have been very true or it might not, but one thing was certain, Thomas Porter had no right to her, and so the invariable result followed—he had to pay a fine. What else ensued we shall never know.

The glimpses we get of the ways and doings of the old stewards of manors are not pleasing; I am afraid that as a class they were hard as nails. Perhaps they could not help themselves, but they certainly very rarely erred on the side of mercy and forbearance. Is not that phrase " making allowances for," a comparatively modern phrase? At any rate the *thing* is not often to be met with in the fourteenth century. Yet in the plague year every now and then one is pleased to find instances actually of consideration for the distress and penury of the homagers at this place and that. Thus at Lessingham, when the worst was over and a court was held on the 15th of January, 1350, the steward writes down that only thirty shillings was to be

levied from the customary tenants by way of tallage,
" Because the greater part of those tenants who
were wont to render tallage had died in the previous
year by reason of the deadly pestilence."

Here and there, too, we come upon heriots
remitted because the heir was so very poor, and
here and there fines and fees are cancelled *causa
miseriæ propter pestilentiam*. Surely it is better to
assume that this kind of thing was done, as our
friend Bonington puts it, *mero motu pietatis suæ* than
because there was no money to be had. Better give
a man the benefit of the doubt, even though he has
been dead five hundred years, than kick him because
he will never tell any more tales.

If it happened sometimes that the plague brought
out the good in a man, sometimes changed his life
from one of covetous indifference or grasping selfishness into a life of earnestness and devout philan-
thropy, it happened at other times—and I fear it
must be confessed more frequently—that coarse
natures, hard and cruel ones, were made more brutal
and callous by the demoralizing influences of that
frightful summer.

I am sure it will be very gratifying to some enlightened and chivalrous people to learn that I have
at least one bad story against a parson.

Here it is !

The rolls of the manor of Waltham show that the plague lingered about there till late in the spring of 1350. As elsewhere, there must needs have been much change in the benefices of the neighbourhood. Of course some of the new parsons were scamps, the laity who survived being, equally of course, models of all that was lovely and estimable. One of these clerical impostors had got a cure somewhere in the neighbourhood—where is not stated, but, inasmuch as his clerical income had not come up to his expectations or his necessities, or his own estimate of his deserts, he found it necessary to supplement that income by somewhat unprofessional conduct. In fact, the Rev. William—that was his name—seems actually to have thrown up his clerical avocations and by his flagrant irregularities had got to himself the notorious sobriquet of William the One-day priest. I should not be surprised to find out that this worthy was captain of a band of robbers who infested Epping Forest. In the end of January, 1351, Matilda, wife of John Clement de Godychester, was quietly riding homewards when, as she passed by the sheepfold of Plesset, out came the Rev. William and bade the lady stand and deliver. Her attendants, it is to be presumed, took to their heels, and the lady, being unable to help herself, delivered up her purse—the account says the Rev. William cut it off—and moreover surrendered a ring of some value, after which she continued her journey. She raised the hue and cry to some purpose, and the clerical king of the road was taken and . . . there is no more. No ! It is a story without an end.

But there were then, as there are now, other ways of preying upon our fellow-creatures and levying blackmail from them, without going to the length of highway robbery—cold work, and a little risky at times.

Henry Anneys, at Lessingham, could work upon the fears of Alice Bakeman and extort a douceur from her without resorting to violence. Mrs. Bakeman had succeeded to the property of some dead kinsman, and Mr. Anneys heard of it. He called on the lady and informed her that for a consideration he would save her from paying any heriot to the lord ; he had certain information which he could use either way. Finally, it was agreed that Alice should give the rogue a cow as hush-money, and with the cow Mr. Anneys departed. His triumph was brief. When the time for holding the next court arrived, others came round the poor woman, and made it quite evident that the lands she had succeeded to were not heriotable at all, and that Henry Anneys was a swindler. So the case was brought before the homage as usual, the cow was ordered to be returned, and a substantial fine imposed upon Anneys.

Almost the first thing that strikes a novice who looks into the village history of the thirteenth and fourteenth centuries is the astounding frequency of bloody quarrels among the rustics. In the records of the Courts Leet for Norfolk it is very seldom indeed, that you can find a court held at which one or more persons, male and female, are not amerced for "drawing blood" from somebody. Whether it was by punching their opponents on the nose, or whether they used their knives, I hesitate to decide; but I suspect, from the frequent mention of knives and daggers, that sticking one's enemy with cold steel was not so very un-English a practice as popular prejudice is wont to assume it to be. One thing is very certain, and that is — that all over East Anglia, five hundred years ago, there was such an amount of bloodletting in village frays as would hardly have disgraced the University of Heidelberg. In Norfolk these sanguinary fights must have been a passion; but one would have thought that, while the plague was raging and after it had begun to subside, then, if ever, men and women would have become less savage and ferocious. So far from it, such records of the years 1349 and 1350 as I have examined are fuller than ever of fights and quarrels,

At Lessingham, about Christmas time, 1349, there was a free fight of a most sanguinary character, men and women joining in it freely. It seems to have arisen from some one finding a horse wandering about the deserted fields. As a stray it belonged to the lord—the finder took a different view, somebody cried " Halves ! " and somebody else said, " I'll give information," and somebody else replied, " So will I," whereupon arose a bloody battle as has been told. About the same time at Hunstanton, Catherine Busgey, evil-disposed old hag that she was, had stript a dead man of his leather jerkin. Did she proceed to wear the manly attire that she might be dagger-proof for the next encounter ? Rash woman ! The dead man's friends recognized the well-known coat, it was forfeited and delivered over to the lord.

It might well be supposed that, while the whole executive machinery of the country was being subject to a tremendous strain, there would be in some districts a condition of affairs which differed very little from downright anarchy. Yet here, again, the existing records are surprisingly free from any evidence tending to support such an assumption. England was not governed by the Home Secretary in those days. Every parish was a living political unit with its own police and its own local government. However desirable it may appear to some to bring back such a state of things, the question nevertheless remains how far it is ever possible to revivify an organization which has long since died a natural death. That, in the fourteenth century, the country districts governed themselves there can be no doubt at all; with what results, as far as the greatest happiness of the greatest number is concerned, this is not the time or the place to inquire or to decide. Yet I cannot withhold my conviction that, if any such gigantic calamity were to fall upon our people now as fell upon them when the Black Death swept over the face of the land five centuries ago—a calamity so sweeping, so overwhelming—its consequences upon the whole social fabric would be incomparably more disastrous than it was in times when centralization was almost unknown and practically impossible. Be it as it may, since the days when the Roman Senate passed a vote of confidence in a beaten general because he had not despaired of the republic, I know nothing in history that impresses a student more profoundly with a sense of the magnificent self-possession, self-control, and self-respect of a suffering nation, under circumstances of unexampled agony and horror, than the simple prosaic annals which remain to us of the great plague year in England.

In only one district in Norfolk have I found evidence of any widespread lawlessness. Even there one hears of it only to hear of vigorous grappling with the ruffians, who were not allowed to have it all their own way.

The hundred of Depwade, lying to the south of Norwich, contains twenty-three parishes; and at the time we are concerned with had very few resident gentry of any consideration. Then, as now, the country parsons were the most important people in the district, and the benefices were above the average in value. In the summer and autumn, at least fifteen of these clergymen fell victims to the plague; among them the rector of Bunwell and the vicar of Tibenham, adjoining parishes. The vicarage was a poor one; it was worth no one's holding; the rectory had been held by William Banyard, a near relative of Sir Robert Banyard, lord of the manor; the plague carried him off in July, and his successor was instituted on the 25th of the month, but does not seem to have come into residence immediately. There had been a clean sweep of the old incumbents from all the parishes for miles round; the poor people, left to themselves, became demoralized; there seems to have been a general scramble, and for a while no redress anywhere. It is recorded that the cattle roamed at will over the standing corn with none to tend them, and that there had been none to make the lord's hay; that among others who had died there were five substantial men among the homagers on whose lands heriots of more or less value were due; but no heriot was recoverable, inasmuch as since the last court certain persons unknown had plundered all that could be carried off —cattle and sheep and horses and goods, and there was nothing to distrain upon but the bare lands and the bare walls.

It may be presumed that where a scoundrel escaped the contagion altogether, while others were dying all round him, or where another recovered after being brought to death's door, in such cases the man would, as a rule, be a person of exceptional strength and vigorous constitution. Such fellows, when the evil spirit was upon them, would be ugly customers to deal with. Gilbert Henry, of Tibenham, was a somewhat audacious thief when he walked into John Smith's house, where there was none alive to bar the door, and carried off certain bushels of malt and barley, with other goods not specified; and, not content therewith, stripped the dead man of his coat and waistcoat. The value of these articles of apparel was not assessed very highly—only sixpence each— and Master Gilbert, after paying the price of the garments, seems to have gone away with them. It is hardly to be wondered at that neither steward nor lord greatly coveted that coat and waistcoat. At the same court, too, William Hessland was amerced for appropriating the few trumpery chattels of Walter Cokstone, a *villein* belonging to the lord. Another wretched pair—a man and his wife—had deliberately cleared a crop of oats off an acre and a half of land, and stacked it in their own barn. Their view was that it belonged to no one; the steward took a different view, and reminded them that what grew on no man's land was the property of some one other than the smart man who ventured to lift it.

It was at Bunwell, too, that William Sigge was by way of becoming a terror to his neighbours. It was laid to his charge, generally, that he had from time to time during the pestilence carried off and appropriated various articles of property (*diversa catalla*) too numerous to specify. They must have been a very miscellaneous lot, for they included several hurdles and the lead stripped off a dead man's roof, not to mention such trifles as garments and pots and pans. Sigge was a very successful plunderer, and his success rather turned his head. When the autumn of 1350 came, he refused to do his autumn service, protested that there was none to do, and was fined accordingly; not only so, but he was found to have stubbed up a hedge which had been the boundary of the land of Robert Attebrigge, who had died with no one to represent him. The women were as bad as the men; they had their rights in those days. One of these beldames was caught walking away with a couple of handmills from a plague-struck dwelling, and another had looted a tenement where John Rucock's corpse lay; she too had stripped the dead!

It is not a little curious to notice how that love of going to law which old Fuller two hundred years ago remarked upon as a characteristic of Norfolk men comes out again when the confusion had begun to subside. The plague is no sooner at an end than the local courts are resorted to for the hearing of every kind of odd question which the complications arising from the abnormal mortality had occasioned.

When Edward Burt died at Lessingham, he left his widow Egidia all he had; but he owed Margery Brown the sum of thirty shillings. Egidia at once provided herself with a second husband, and surrendered herself and her belongings to Edward Bunting. Mrs. Brown applied for her little bill. Egidia, now no longer a widow, but lawful wife of Mr. Bunting, repudiated the debt; she was widow no longer, she had become the property of another man; the debt, she pleaded, was buried in her first husband's grave. That little quibble was soon overruled. But there were often cases which were by no means so

easily disposed of. Robert Bokenham was lord of
the manor of Tibenham, and Robert Tate was one
of his tenants. Tate died; then Bokenham died.
Bokenham's son was only nine years old, and no
guardian had been appointed when Tate's son died.
Then followed a dispute as to who was guardian of
young Bokenham, and of whom Tate's land was
held, and who was the true heir. A pleasant little
brief there for a rising barrister to hold.

A complication of much the same kind arose at
Croxton. William Galion, a man of some consideration, died in July, leaving his wife Beatrix with two
sons; but he died intestate. Beatrix had just time
to pay a heavy fine to the lord for the privilege of
being her eldest son's guardian when the plague took
her. Before she died she left the guardianship of
her first-born son John to her husband's brother
Adam; a few days afterwards the boy John died, and
his brother Robert alone remained; the guardianship
of the boy John is of course at an end, and uncle
Adam applies for the guardianship of the surviving
nephew; but by this time he is unable to find the
money; whereupon the child's estate is taken into
the hands of the lord till such time as the uncle can
pay the fees demanded.

Walter Wyninge had a wise woman for his wife,
and her name was Matilda. The Black Death left her

a widow, but she speedily married without any license from the lord to William Oberward. The second husband had a very brief enjoyment of his married life; in a few days he too died, and Matilda married a third husband, one Peter the carpenter. At this point Matilda's turn came and she died. All this had happened in the interval of two months since the last manor court was held. The steward of the manor claimed a heriot from Wyninge's land and another from Oberward's. But the astute Peter was equal to the occasion : he pleaded that, according to the custom of the manor, no heriot could be levied from a widow till she had survived her husband a year and a day, and he demanded that the court rolls should be searched to confirm or correct his assertion. I suspect he knew his business, and no heriot came to that grasping steward. Who pities him ?

Ladies and gentlemen of the romantic order of mind will be shocked at the indelicacy of Mistress Matilda—she of the many names. I suspect that they would be shocked by a great many things in the domestic life of England five centuries ago. Marrying for love has a sweet sound about it, but the thing did not exist in the old days. When did it exist ? History is very hard upon romance; History, disdaining courtesy, lifts one veil after another, opens closed doors, reveals long-buried secrets, turns her bull's-eye upon the dark corners, and breaks the old seals. She is very cynical, and will by no means side with this appellant or with that. Beautiful theories crumble into dust when they stand before her judgment-seat, and old dreams, offspring of brains that were wrestling with slumber in the darkness, pass away as the dawn comes, bringing with it, too often, such revelations as are not altogether lovely to dwell on. In the fourteenth century an unmarried woman was a chattel, and belonged to somebody who had the right to sell her or to give her away. That is the naked truth. You may make a man an offender for a word if you will, and object that " sell " is an incorrect term ; but the fact remains, however much some may—

> leave the sense their learning to display,
> And some explain the meaning quite away.

Hence, when a wretched woman was mourning alone over the husband who had just been hustled into his grave, the men were after her like wolves, every one of her neighbours knowing exactly what she was worth even to the fraction of a rood of land, or the last lamb that had been dropped, or the litter of pigs that were rootling up the beech-nuts in the woods. They gave her short time to make up her mind. Sentiment ? We in the East—the land of the wise men since time was young—we know nothing of sentiment. We can hate with a sullen tenacity of resentment which knows no forgiveness; but love—nay we leave that for the "intense" of other climes. And women in the good old times—positively women—love one man more than another? What *they?*

> "Whose love knows no distinction but of gender,
>   And ridicules the very name of choice!"

Why, where were you born?

The records of the marriages on the court rolls of the plague year are hardly more startling than the deaths. Whether men and women paid less to the lord for a license than they were compelled to pay if they married without license I cannot tell; but that hundreds of widows must have married only a few weeks or a few days after their husbands' deaths is clear. Matilda's case was not a rare one. Alice Foghal, at Lessingham, was another of those ladies who in a couple of months had been the property successively of three husbands—the last was actually a stranger. Where he came from is not stated, but he sate himself down by the widow's hearth, claimed it as his own, and paid a double fee for his successful gallantry. How he managed the matter remains unexplained, but young brides were plentiful in the parish just about that time; and at the same court where Alice's matrimonial alliances were compounded for, no less than fifteen other young women paid their fees for marrying without license from the lord. I have only noticed one instance of anything like remission of *marriage fees*, though I hope it was less uncommon than appears on the rolls. The lady in this case was a butcher's widow, and it was too much to expect that she could wait till the next court, wherefore the steward graciously knocked off seventy-five per cent. of his due; and, in lieu of two shillings, charged her only sixpence—*ratione temporis et in misericordia*, as he sententiously observes. Magnanimous steward!

I have met with no evidence leading to the belief that anywhere in the country villages there was anything approaching to a panic. Only a novice would be led astray by what he might read occurred at Coltishall. Five brothers named Gritlof and two other brothers named Primrose, being *nativi*, i.e., *villeins born*, and so the property of the lord, had decamped whither none could tell; the court solemnly adjudicated upon the case, and decreed that the seven runaways should be attached *per corpora*, whatever that may mean. But Coltishall is barely five miles from Norwich, and from the villages round the great city the *villeins* were always running away in the hopes of getting their freedom if they could keep in hiding within the city walls for a year and a day Oh, ye seven, had the yellow primrose less charm for you, and the barley loaves that were sure for you in breezy Coltishall—gritty though they might be—less charm than the garbage that might be picked up in Norwich, in its noisome alleys reeking with corruption, and all that flesh and blood revolts from? Ah! but to be free—to be free! How that thought made their poor hearts throb!

That there was panic—mad, unreasoning, insensate panic—elsewhere than in the country villages there is abundant evidence to prove, but it was among the well-to-do classes—the traders and the moneyed men, *bourgeoisie* of the towns—that a stampede prevailed. Any one who chooses may satisfy himself of this by looking into Rymer's *Fœdera*, to go no further

. . . . . .

Enough has been told in the foregoing pages to illustrate the overwhelming violence with which the Great Plague ran its career in East Anglia. Only a small part of the evidence still ready to our hands has been examined; but if no more were scrutinized, the impression left upon us of the severity of the visitation would be quite sufficiently appalling. It is, however, when an attempt to estimate the immediate effects and the remoter consequencs that followed that our difficulties begin.

Before a man is qualified to dogmatize upon those

effects, he must have gone some way towards making himself familiar with the social and economic conditions of the country during at least the century before the plague. Unfortunately the history of economics in England has never been attempted by any one at all duly qualified for dealing with so complex and difficult a subject, and the crudest theories have been substituted for sound conclusions, then only to be accepted when based upon the solid ground of ascertained fact. In the childhood of every science dogmatism precedes induction, and in the absence of clear knowledge, foolish and wild-eyed visionaries have posed as discoverers again and again. Yet bluster and audacity have their use, if only to stimulate the timid and the dilatory to quicken their pace and move forwards. For my part, however, if it be necessary to choose between the two, I should prefer to err with the slow and cautious rather than with the rash and over-bold; the former may for a while serve as a drag upon the chariot wheels of progress, the latter are sure to thrust us out of the road and land us at last in some quagmire whence it will be very hard to get back into the right track.

The great teacher who, with his transcendent genius, has done more to create a school of English history than all who have gone before him, who, in fact, has made English history, not what it is, but what it will be, when his influence shall have permeated our literature, has spoken on this subject of the Black Death with his usual profound suggestiveness. The Bishop of Chester looks with grave distrust upon any theory which ascribes to the Great Plague as a cause " nearly all the social changes which take place in England down to the Reformation: the depopulation of towns, the relaxation of the bonds of moral and social law, the solution of the continuity of national development caused by a sort of disintegration in society generally." [1] And yet this appalling visitation must have constituted a very important factor in the working out of those social and political problems with which the life of every great nation is concerned. Such problems, however, are not simple ones; rather they are infinitely complex; and he who would set himself to analyse the processes by which the ultimate results are arrived at will blunder hopelessly if he takes account of only a single unknown quantity.

1. It is obvious that the sudden exhaustion of the large reserve force of clergy must have made itself felt at once in every parish in England. In the diocese of Norwich a considerable number of the parsons who died belonged to the gentry class. Then, as now,

---

[1] " Constitutional History," vol. ii. chap. xvi. p. 399, § 259, edit. 1875.

there were family livings to which younger sons might hope to be presented, and were presented, as vacancies occurred ; but, in the face of the sudden and widely extended mortality, it was inevitable that appointments should be made with very little reference to a man's social grade or intellectual proficiency. Patrons had to take whom they could get. This of itself would tend to a deterioration in the character of the clergy; but this was not all. The clergy died ; but other holders of offices, civil and ecclesiastical, were not spared. There was a sudden opening out of careers in every direction for the ambitious and the unemployed : young men who ten years before would never have dreamt of anything but "resorting to holy orders," turned their eyes to other walks and adopted other views ; and it is plain that a large number of those who presented themselves for admission to the clerical profession as we now understand it, in many instances belonged to a lower class than their predecessors. Some were devout and earnest, such country parsons as Chaucer described—he does not turn aside to caricature *them* —but others were mere adventurers, hirelings whose heart was not in their work. These clerical scamps gave Archbishop Simon Islip a great deal of trouble. The smaller livings were forsaken, the curate market rose, the chaplains would neither take the country vicarages nor engage themselves as regular helpers to the parish priests. London swarmed with itinerants who preferred picking up a livelihood by occasional duty, when they could make their own terms, to binding themselves to a cure of souls.[1] The primate denounced these greedy ones again and again, but it was all in vain ; the bishops found it impossible to draw the reins of discipline as tightly as they wished, and found it equally impossible to prevent the extortionate demands of such curates as could be got. The evil grew to such a height that the faithful Commons took the matter up and petitioned the King to interfere, inasmuch as "les chappeleins sont devenuz si chers" that they actually demanded ten or even twelve marks a year as their stipend—"a grant grevance & oppression du poeple." The usual methods were resorted to, and if people could be made good by Act of Parliament the evils complained of would have disappeared. They did not disappear, and the evil grew. Unhappily the increased stipends did not serve to produce a better

---

[1] Compare Chaucer's words—

> "He sette not his benefice to hire,
> And lette his sheep accombred in the mire,
> *And ran unto London, into Seint Paules*
> *To seken him a chanterie for Soules"*——

with Wilkins' "Concilia," vol. iii. 1.

I

article, and it is only too plain that the religious convictions and the religious life of the people suffered seriously. Ten years after the Black Death the Archbishop expresses his deep sorrow at the neglect of Sunday, the desertion of the churches and the decline in religious observances. Yet we must be cautious how we attribute this break-up in the old habits of the people to the plague exclusively, or even mainly. Some of the evils complained of had already begun to be felt before the plague came, and may fairly be attributed, not to the falling short of the numbers of the clergy, but exactly the reverse.

Already a strong reaction had set in against the friars, their influence and their teaching had begun to be regarded as menacing to the stability of existing creeds and existing institutions. Langland hated them. Chaucer held them up to scorn. Wickliffe denounced them with a righteous wrath. Fitz-Ralph, Archbishop of Armagh, carried on open war against them. All these leaders of the chosen bands that fight the battles of God had arrived at man's estate when the Black Death came, and all survived it. They certainly were not the product of the great visitation ; they were the spokesmen and representatives of a generation that had begun to look at the world with larger, other eyes than their fathers. That which was coming would have come if there had been no plague at all, and so far from its being certain that that calamity was in any great degree the cause of the upheaval that ensued, it is at least as probable that the sudden decrease in the population served to retard the action of forces already working mightily in the direction of revolution—revolution it might be for the better, or it might be for the worse.

2. Whoever else may have been losers or sufferers by the plague, there was one class which emerged from that dreadful year very much richer than before. The lords of the manors, the representatives of what we now call the country gentry, were great gainers. Not only did the extraordinary amount paid in heriots and fees make up an aggregate which in itself constituted a very large percentage upon the capital embarked in agriculture, but the extent of land which *escheated* to the lords was very considerable. Moreover, the manors themselves, or as we should say, the landed property of the country, came into fewer hands; the gentry became richer and their estates larger. Knighton draws attention to the fact that in the towns a large number of houses became ruinous for want of occupants, but he adds that in the hamlets and villages the same effects followed, and that everywhere. Here again, the rolls of Parliament corroborate the assertion and in.

form us that not only the dwellings of the homagers but the capital mansions themselves, were deserted and falling to decay. When, in the next reign, the manor of Hockham came into the possession of Richard, Earl of Arundel, in right of his wife, he took the precaution of having a careful survey made of the condition of the estate as it came into his hands. The manor-house had not been tenanted for thirty years. It had been a mansion of considerable pretension and two stories high; on the ground-floor the doors were all gone; on the upper floor the windows were open to the air; the chamber "vocata ladyes chambre" was roofless, the offices were too dilapidated to be worth repair. The enclosing walls and the moat had been utterly neglected. The offices had formerly been adapted for a large establishment; there had been extensive farm buildings, and at least six substantial houses for the bailiff and other farm servants. Among other buildings there were two *fishouses* built of timber and *daubur*, in which apparently the keeper of the fishponds lived, and some elaborate arrangements had existed for keeping up the supply of fish in the ponds by methods of pisciculture to us unknown. The windmill had long ceased to be used, its very grinding stones had disappeared. Worse than all, there was no more any gallows or pillory, or even stocks, *pro libertate servanda,* as the jurors quaintly remark. Yet the records show that at Hockham things had gone on pretty much as before since the big house was deserted. The courts were held with exemplary regularity, the fees had been exacted with unwavering rigour, the homagers settled their own affairs in their own way; but there was this difference, that for a generation the tenants had been living under an absentee landlord, who so far from being the poorer because the big house had been tumbling down, was the richer, inasmuch as he had one mansion the less to keep up out of his income. What happened at Hockham must have happened in hundreds of other parishes; there must have been large tracts of country during the latter half of the reign of Edward the Third where a resident landlord was the exception to that which aforetime had been the rule.

. . . . . .

3. In the present condition of our knowledge, any estimate of the actual numbers who perished in the plague must be the merest guesswork. It may be that two millions were carried off; it may be there were three. It is undeniable that a very large proportion of the inhabitants of this island died in a few months—employers and employed. We must, however, remember that England in the fourteenth century was incomparably more self-supporting than

it is in the nineteenth century; that there were no great centres of industry then; that the rural population was largely in excess of the urban population; that we exported the wool which the Flemings manufactured into cloth; and that if there were fewer hands to till the soil, there were fewer mouths to feed. No one can doubt that the labour market must have been seriously disturbed, but it is very easy to exaggerate this disturbance; and whether it were less or more than has been asserted, we shall certainly err by attributing the rise in wages, which undoubtedly took place after the Black Death, to it, and to it alone—*post hoc ergo propter hoc* is not a safe conclusion. Granted, as we must grant, that the plague accelerated the rise in wages, it is certain the upward movement had already begun before the population had been seriously lessened. The number of clergy, to be sure, was largely in excess of the needs of the country; the clerical profession had become "choked" by the influx of young men presumably with *some* private means to fall back upon; among them there must have been, and there was, serious competition for every vacant post. When the reserve of supernumeraries became absorbed, the competition turned the other way, and the surviving clergy could make their own terms. It was otherwise with the masses, especially with the peasantry. If there were an insufficient number of labourers to till the land heretofore in cultivation, the worst land fell out of cultivation, and no one was much the worse. It was all very well for some landlords to complain that their rents had fallen off. Yes! Then—as now, as always—the small proprietors suffered severely, and needy men are wont to be clamorous. Then—as now, as always—the sufferers looked about them for a cause of their distress, and found it in any event that was nearest at hand. But we know that the style of living after the plague was incomparably more luxurious and extravagant than it was before. The country was producing less, it may be; but the people, man for man, were much richer than before.

When we find ourselves confronted with the rhetorical stuff which the literature of preambles and parliamentary petitions in the fourteenth century flaunts so liberally before our eyes, we must learn to accept the statements of draughtsmen *cum grano,* and to read between the lines. The Commons were quite equal to making the most of any calamity that occurred. When the Parliament, which had not met since mid Lent, 1348, assembled once more in February, 1350, the plague was not forgotten. In the petitions presented to the King, the havoc wrought is dwelt upon and deplored, *not* with a view to remedy any of the distress that had ensued, but in the hope that the arrears of taxation due from the dead might be excused to the survivors who had succeeded to the others' property. If they complain of the scarcity and dearness of corn, this is to give point to their protest against the King's servants taking it for the victualling of his army and the town of Calais. If, again, they sound a note of alarm at the outrageous insolence of the labourers who presumed to demand a large increase of wage, and would not work at the old scale of pay, there is no pretence that the employers could not afford to accede to the increased demand; the "grand meschief du poeple" consisted in this, that the tillers of the soil should have dreamt of asserting themselves in any way whatever. Moreover, when it came to legislating against the mutinous labourers, King and Parliament, while sternly setting their faces against the rise in wages, *do not take the twenty-third year of the King as the standard year* by which to settle what the normal rate of wages should be. They go back to the twentieth year, *ou cynk ou sis ans devans.* That is to say, the wages had been steadily rising for ten years before the plague; the labourers had been getting their share of the increased prosperity of the country; and the Statute of Labourers was only one of the clumsy attempts to interfere with the action of a great economical law which had been working silently for the advantage of the operatives long before the Black Death had come to perplex and confuse men's minds and disturb their calculations.

.   .   .   .   .   .

Some of us remember when the science of geology was young—and we were young too—we remember how there was a certain romance and fascination about those fearless and richly imaginative theories which explained all the great changes in the crust of the earth by magnificent cataclysms, upheaving, exploding, overwhelming. The crack of doom meant something after all! What had been should be again. Old times had stories to tell of sublime catastrophes, the crash of systems, and the swallowing up of chains of cloud-capped mountains in the yawning abysses of a world that might at any moment turn itself inside out. Alas! the cataclysm theories had to die the death, and we had to comfort ourselves with a dull prosaic dream of forces acting with infinite slowness, grinding, and evolving through unnumbered ages, the great laws working themselves out without haste or any tendency to those picturesque paroxysms which have a certain charm for us in our nonage. When Sociology shall have risen to the dignity of a science—and that day may come—

I 2

I think she too will be chary of resorting to the cataclysm theory; she and her handmaid History will hardly smile approval upon pretenders who are anxious to discover a single efficient cause for results which a million influences have combined to bring about, or who assume that every new phenomenon must disturb the equilibrium of the world. To take up with theories first in the hope, and sometimes with the determination, that facts shall be found to support them at last, is the vice—I had almost said the crime—of too many of those who now are styled historians.

If at this point I leave to others the further pursuit of a subject which deserves a more comprehensive treatment than it has yet received, it is not because I have not much more that I could tell. If it be true that the proper study of mankind is man, it is at least as true that the proper study of Englishmen is the history of England; that, however, means a great deal more than is usually understood by the words. It means the history of English institutions, of the social, the intellectual, and the religious life of our forefathers—it means a great deal more than the life of our sovereigns, their wars, their virtues or their follies. Unhappily historic studies in England, notwithstanding the splendid impetus that has been given to them of late by the brilliant achievements of some philosophic enquirers, receive but scant encouragement, and for the most part a man's labour must be his own reward. In our elementary schools History is almost utterly ignored. A whole people is rapidly breaking with the past from sheer ignorance that there is any past that is worth knowing. Who shall estimate the immeasurable harm that must be wrought to a nation that has lost touch with the past? Let men but believe, to their shame, that

> The glories of our birth and state
> Are shadows, not substantial things,

and what becomes of patriotism? Granted, if you will, that English history has been made too often a dry and repulsive study by those who have undertaken to teach it and write it; need it remain so? It must remain so as long as we keep to the old lines and content ourselves with the old methods. What is wanted to make any science *interesting* is that it should push its inquiries into new fields of research. The means and appliances, and opportunities for pursuing historical researches open to those whose youth is not all behind them, are such as we, their seniors, never dreamt of when we were in our early manhood. There are whole worlds as yet unexplored and waiting to be won. Do men whimperingly complain that there is no longer a career for genius? Tush! It is enthusiasm that is wanted. Give us that, and the career will follow. But the enthusiasm must be of the real sort—not self-asserting, self-conscious, self-seeking; but earnest, patient, resolute, and reticent : for science, too, needs heroism no less than war.

In the domain of Physical Science there has been in our own time no lack of intelligent co-operation, and volunteers have been many and earnest, nor have they spared themselves or shrunk from sacrifices. In the domain of Historical Science the labourers are few and far between; there research proceeds with lagging steps. No one sneers at a philosopher who travels to Iceland to investigate the habits of a gnat, or who counts it the pride of his life to have discovered a new fungus, but simpletons are pleased to make themselves merry with caricaturing any student of his country's institutions who is "always poring over musty old parchments." And yet these minute researches will have to be made sooner or later, and till we can bring ourselves to study the structure and the tissues and the comparative anatomy of Institutions, and to go through all the drudgery which sluggards loathe and fools deride, the light of truth will be dim for us all; our Ethical, equally with our political Philosophy must remain in a condition of hopeless sterility. Nevertheless History too has her mission, though her time has not yet come. It will not always be that the past will be to us " as the words of a book that is sealed, which men deliver to one that is learned, saying, Read this, I pray thee : and he saith I cannot, for it is sealed ; and the book is delivered to him that is not learned, saying, Read this, I pray thee : and he saith, I am not learned."

No ! It will not be always so.

VI

*THE BUILDING UP OF A UNIVER-
SITY.*

. . . . "so famous,
So excellent in art, and still so rising."

SOME years ago I found myself in a Northern capital,
and committed myself to the guidance of a native
coachman, whose business and pride it was to drive
me from place to place, and indicate to me the important buildings of his majestic city. He was a
patriotic showman, and I am bound to say he showed
us a great deal; but the most memorable moment of
that instructive day was when he stopped before,
what seemed to us, a respectable mansion in a respectable street, and announced to us that "*yon*"
was "the Free Kirk *Univairsity.*" It was the first
time in my life that I had heard four stone walls
with a roof over them called a University. It was
not long, however, before I discovered that I myself

had been living with my head in a sack and, in more senses than one, had been of those

> Who sweep the crossings, wet or dry,
> And all the world go by them.

Only so could it have come to pass that this new meaning for an old word had struck me as strange, not to say ludicrous.

> Licuit semperque licebit
> Signatum præsente nota producere nomen.

Allowable? Yes! and much more than merely allowable; it is inevitable that as the ages roll we should attach new meanings to old words. And if this is inevitable, not the less inevitable is it that, when we desire to trace the history of the thing signified, we should be compelled to recur to the original meaning of the name by which the thing is designated.

A word at starting upon the remarkable book [1] which has suggested the following article. To say of it that it is quite the most sumptuous work that

---

[1] "The Architectural History of the University of Cambridge, and of the Colleges of Cambridge and Eton." By the late Robert Willis, M.A., F.R.S. Edited, with large additions, and brought up to the present time, by John Willis Clark, M.A., late Fellow of Trin. Coll., Camb. 4 vols. super-royal 8vo Cambridge: The University Press.

has ever proceeded from the Cambridge Press, is to say little. It is hardly too much to say that it is one of the most important contributions to the social and intellectual history of England which has ever been made by a Cambridge man. The title of the work conveys but a very inadequate notion of its wide scope, of the encyclopædic learning and originality of treatment which it displays, and, least of all, of the abundance of *human interest* which characterizes it so markedly. It is because of this wealth of human interest that the book must needs exercise a powerful fascination upon those who have a craving to get some insight into the life of their forefathers; and it is because I believe the number of such students of history is in our times rapidly on the increase, that I am anxious to draw attention to some few of the many matters treated of so ably in these magnificent volumes.

.   .   .   .   .   .

The term *University*, in its original acceptation, was used to designate any aggregate of *persons* associated in a political, religious, or trading corporation, having common interests, common privileges, and common property. The inhabitants of a town, the members of a fraternity, the brethren of a guild, the monks or canons of a religious house, when addressed in formal instruments, were addressed as a

University. Nay! when the whole body of the faithful is appealed to as Christian men, the ordinary phrase made use of by lay or ecclesiastical potentate, when signifying his wishes or intentions, is " Noverit *Universitas* vestra." A University in this sense, regarded as an aggregate of persons, might be localized or it might not; its members might be scattered over the whole Christian world, or they might constitute an inner circle of some larger community, of which they—though a *Universitas*—formed but a part. A University in its original signification meant no more than our modern term an Association. When men associated together for purposes of trade, they were a trading *Universitas;* when they associated for religious objects, they were a religious *Universitas;* when they associated for the promotion of learning, they were a learned *Universitas.* But the men came first, the bricks and mortar followed long after. The architectural history, in its merely technical and professional details, could only start at a point where the University, as an association of scholars and students, had already acquired power and influence, had been at work for long, and had got to make itself felt as a living force in the body politic and in the national life. It was because the antiquaries of a former age lost sight of this truth that they indulged in the extravagances they did. Starting from the assumption that stone walls make an institution, they professed to tell when the Universities came into existence and who were their earliest founders. The authors of this modern *Magnum Opus* have set themselves to deal with a far more instructive problem. Their object has been to trace the growth of the University of to-day in its concrete form, down from the early times when it existed only in the germ ; and to show us how " the glorious fellowship of living men," which constituted the *personal* University of the eleventh or the twelfth century, developed by slow degrees into the brick-and-mortar Universities of the nineteenth—such Universities as are springing up all over the world ; their teachers advertised for in *The Times*, and their students tempted to come and be taught in them by the bait of money rewards.

.   .   .   .   .   .

As to the exact time when a band of scholars and teachers first made their home in Cambridge or Oxford, and began to attract to themselves from the four winds classes of eager youths hungry for intellectual food and anxious to listen and learn, that we must be content to leave undetermined. They who like the flavour of the old antiquarianism may enjoy it in its spiciest form, if they choose to hunt up among certain forgotten volumes now grown scarce. They may read what John Caius (pronounced Keys) wrote as the champion of Cambridge, and Thomas Caius wrote as champion of Oxford ; they may rejoice their hearts over the Battle of the Keys, and come to what conclusion they prefer to arrive at. For most of us, however, this sort of old-world lore has lost its charm. A man lives through his taste for some questions. The student of history nowadays is inclined to say with St. Paul, " So fight I not as one that beateth the air," and to reject with some impatience the frivolous questions which help not a jot towards bringing us into closer relation with the life and personality of our ancestors.

> " I am half sick of shadows," said
> The Lady of Shalott ;

and we, too, have grown weary of weaving our webs with our backs to the light. There is no making any way in Cloudland. We ask for firm ground on which to plant our footsteps, if we would move onwards.

. . . . . .

It would have been very galling to the Oxford antiquaries of Queen Elizabeth's days to have to acknowledge that there was a Cambridge before there was an Oxford. Nevertheless the fact is so. Hide your diminished heads, ye rash ones who would fain have us believe that a thousand years before our era, King

Mempric, the wicked king whom the wolves ate—as was right and fitting they should—built a noble city, which as time went on " was called *Oxonia*, or by the Saxons *Oxenfordia*." Alack! it turns out that we must make an enormous step along the course of time before we can find trace of any such city or anything like it. It turns out that " the year 912 saw Oxford made a fortified town, with a definite duty to perform and a definite district assigned to it." What! Seven years after the great Alfred had closed his eyes in death, and left to others the work which he had showed them how to do? Yes! Even so. It may be very hard to have to confess the odious crime of youth; but it seems almost capable of demonstration that Cambridge, as a fortress and a a town existed a thousand years before Oxford was anything but a desolate swamp, or at most a trumpery village, where a handful of Britons speared eels, hunted for deer, and laboriously manufactured earthenware pots. What have we to do with thee, thou daughter of yesterday? Stand aside while thine elder sister—ay, old enough to be thy mother —takes her place of honour. She has waited long for her historian; he has come at last, and he was worth waiting for.

In times before the Roman legionaries planted their firm feet in Britain, there was a very formidable fortress at Cambridge. It contained about sixty acres; it was surmounted by one of those mighty earthworks which the hand of man in the old days raised by sheer brute force, or rather by enormous triumph of organized labour. The Romans drove out the Britons, and settled a garrison in the place. Two of the great Roman roads intersected at this point, and the conquerors called it by a new name, as was their wont, retaining some portion of the old one. In their language it was known as *Camboritum.* The primeval fortress stood on the left bank of the river, which some called the Granta and some called the Cam; and for reasons best known to themselves, the Romans did not think fit to span that river by a bridge, but they made their great Via Devana pass sheer through the river—as some Dutch or German Irrationalist has pretended that the children of Israel did when they found the Jordan barring their progress —that is, those Roman creatures constructed a solid pavement in the bed of the sluggish stream, over which less audacious engineers would have thrown an arch. Through the water they carried a kind of causeway, and the name of the place for centuries indicated that it was situated on the *ford* of the Cam. But what the Roman did not choose to do, that the people that came after him found it needful to do. In the Saxon Chronicle we find that the old fortress which the Romans had held and strengthened, and then perforce abandoned, had got to be called Granta-brygge; and this name, or something very like it, it retained when the great survey was made as the Norman Conqueror's reign was drawing to its close. By this time the town had moved across to the right bank of the river, and had become a town surrounded by a ditch and defended by walls and gates. Already it contained at least four hundred houses, and on the site of the old mound the Norman raised a new castle, and in doing that he laid some twenty-nine houses low.

The early history of Oxford is more or less connected with that of the obscure and insignificant monastery of St. Frideswide, though even at Oxford it is observable that the town and the University grew up in almost entire independence of any influence exercised by any of the older religious houses. At Cambridge this was much more the case. There were no *monks* at Cambridge at any time; there never were any nearer than at the Abbey of Ely, in the old times a long day's journey off, and accessible in the winter, if accessible at all, only by water. King Knut, we are told, greatly favoured the Abbey of Ely, visited it, was entertained there, in fact restored it. But at Cambridge there were no monks. No *real* monks; a fact which ought to be a signifi-

cant hint to "all educated men," but which, unhappily, is likely to be significant only to the few
who have taken the trouble to learn what a real monk
professed to be. If there were no monks at Cambridge, there was something else. Outside the walls
of the town there rose up, in the twelfth century,
the priory of Barnwell—a priory of Augustinian
canons ; and, moreover, a nunnery—the Benedictine
nunnery of St. Rhadegunda. Within the walls there
was another house of Augustinians, which was
known as St. John's Hospital ; that is, a house
where the canons made it part of their duty to
provide a spurious kind of *hospitality* to travellers,
much in the same way that the Hospice of St.
Bernard offers food and shelter now to the wayfarer,
and with such food and shelter something more—to
wit, the opportunity of worshipping the Most High
in peace, up there among the eternal snows. At St.
John's Hospital, as at St. Bernard's, the grateful
wanderer who had found a refuge would leave behind
him his thankoffering in recognition of the kindly
treatment he had met with, and it might happen that
these free gifts constituted no small portion of the
income on which the canons—for the most part a
humble and unpretentious set of men—kept up their
houses.

With the dawn of the thirteenth century came the

great revivalists—the friars. Wherever the friars established themselves they began not only to preach, but to teach. They were the awakeners of a new intellectual life; not only the stimulators of an emotional pietism always prone to run into religious intoxication and extravagance. With the coming of the friars what may be called the modern history of Cambridge begins. Not that it can be allowed that there were no schools of repute on the banks of the Cam till the coming of the friars; it is certain that learning had her home at Cambridge long before this time.

As early as 1187 Giraldus Cambrensis came to Oxford and read his *Expugnatio Hiberniæ* in public lectures, and entertained the doctors of the diverse faculties and the most distinguished scholars.[1] Oxford was doubtless at that time more renowned, but Cambridge followed not far behind. If the friars settled at Cambridge early in their career, it was because there was a suitable home for them there— an opening as we say—which the flourishing condition of the University afforded. There were scholars to teach, there were masters to dispute with, there were doctors to criticize, oppose, or befriend. Doubtless, too, there were already strained relations between the

[1] Bishop Stubbs's " Lectures on Mediæval and Modern History," p. 141, 8vo, 1886.

townsmen and the gownsmen at Cambridge as at Oxford. The first great "town and gown row" which we hear of took place at Oxford in 1209, but when we do hear of it we find the other University mentioned by the historian in close connection with the event recorded. The townsmen under great provocation had seized three of the gownsmen *in hospitio suo* and threw them into the gaol. King John came down to make inquiry, and he hung those three, guiltless though they were, as Matthew Paris assures us. Hereupon there was intense indignation, and the University dispersed. Three thousand of the gownsmen migrated elsewhere, some to Cambridge we learn. Oxford for a while was deserted. This was fifteen years before the Franciscans settled among us. It was the year in which King John was excommunicated. There were only three bishops left in England; the king had worried all the rest away. There was misery and anarchy everywhere. Yet, strange to say, in the midst of all the bitterness men *would* have their sons educated, and the Universities did not despair of the republic. Shadowy and fragmentary as all the evidence is on which we have to rely for the history of the Universities during the twelfth century, it is enough to make us certain that the friars settled at Cambridge because there they found scope for their labours. There was undoubtedly a University there long before they arrived. Nevertheless, it is not till the middle of the reign of Henry the Third (A.D. 1216–1272) that we come upon any direct mention of a corporation which could be regarded as a chartered society of scholars at Cambridge, and it is difficult to resist the conviction that, whatever may have been its previous history, and however far back its infancy may date, the friars were to some extent nursing fathers of the University of Cambridge.

And this brings us again to the point from which we started a page or two back, and gives me the opportunity of quoting a passage from Professor Willis's introduction, which will serve at once as a continuation of and comment upon what has been said, while leading us on to what still lies before us.

The University of the Middle Ages was a corporation of learned men, associated for the purposes of teaching, and possessing the privilege that no one should be allowed to teach within their dominion unless he had received their sanction, which could only be granted after trial of his ability. The test applied consisted of examinations and public disputations; the sanction assumed the form of a public ceremony, and the name of *a degree;* and the teachers or doctors so elected or created carried out their office of instruction by lecturing in the public schools to the students who, desirous of hearing them, took up their residence in the place wherein the University was located. The degree was in fact merely a license to teach; the teacher so licensed became a member of the ruling body.

We have arrived at this point—we find ourselves at the beginning of the thirteenth century face to face with a *University* at Cambridge, a University which, existing originally in its inchoate condition of an association vaguely aiming at the improvement of the methods of education and the encouragement of scholars, had gradually grown into a recognized and powerful body, with direct influence and control over its members ; a body, too, which had become so identified with the interests of culture and research that a change had already begun in the generally received acceptation of its name, and already the word "university" had begun to be restricted to such a *Universitas* as was identified with the life and pursuits of learning and learned men. This means that, *pari passu* with its increase in power, the University had grown too, in the number of its members —the teachers and the taught. The time had arrived when the demands of professors and students for adequate accommodation would become pressing. Lecturers with popular gifts would expect a hall capable of holding their audiences. Public disputations could not be held in a corner. Receptions of eminent scholars from a distance, and all those ceremonials which were so dear to gentle and simple in the middle ages, required space, and were the more effective the grander the buildings in which they were displayed. Yet how little the Cantabs of the thirteenth century could have dreamt of what was coming! What a day of small things it was! Six hundred years ago the giant was in his cradle.

Meanwhile, another need than that of mere schools and lecture-halls had begun to be felt. The scholars who came for what they could get from the teachers —the regents and the doctors—flocked from various quarters; they were young, they were not all fired with the student's love of learning; they were sometimes noisy, sometimes frolicsome, sometimes vicious. As now is the case at Edinburgh and Heidelberg, so it was then at Cambridge, the bonds of discipline were very slight; the scholars had to take their chance; they lodged where they could, they lived anyhow, each according to his means; they were homeless. It was inevitable that all sorts of grave evils should arise.

The lads—they were mere boys—got into mischief, they got into debt with the Jews; for there were Jews at Cambridge, not a few; they were preyed upon by sharpers, were fleeced on the right hand and on the left; many of them learned more harm than good. The elder men, and they who had consciences and hearts, shook their heads, and asked what could be done? For a long time the principle of *laissez faire* prevailed: the young fellows were left to the tender mercies of the townsfolk. There was no grandmotherly legislation in those days. Gradually a kind of joint-stock arrangement came into vogue. Worthy people seemed to have hired a house which they called a *hostel* or hall, and sub-let the rooms to the young fellows; the arrangement appears to have been clumsily managed, and led to dissensions between town and gown; the townsmen soon discovered that the gownsmen were gainers by the new plan, and they themselves were losers. They grumbled, protested, quarrelled. But it was a move in the right direction, and a beginning of some moral discipline was made, and that could not but be well. These *hostels* were set up at Cambridge certainly at the beginning of the thirteenth century, and how long before we cannot tell; but it was at Oxford that the first *college*, as we uuderstand the term, rose into being. It was Walter de Merton, Chancellor of England, who was the father of the collegiate system in England. So far from embarking upon a new experiment without careful deliberation, he spent twelve years of his life in working out his ideas and in elaborating the famous *Rule of Merton*, of which it is not at all too much to say that its publication constituted an era in the history of education and learning in England. Merton died in 1277. Hugh de Balsham, Bishop of

Ely, who survived him nine years, appears to have been moved with a desire to do for Cambridge what Merton had done for Oxford. Balsham is spoken of as the founder of St. Peter's College, and in one sense he was so. The bishops of Ely were the patrons of Cambridge. Bishop Balsham asked himself what could be done, and set himself to deal with the problems which presented themselves for solution in the condition of his own University. He was not a great man, that seems clear enough : his schemes were crude ; he bungled. The truth seems to me to be that the feeling at Cambridge was one of suspicion, and there are indications that the bishops of Ely in an awkward fashion were opposed to anything like *secular education*. We hear of money being left to support *priests* studying theology, and of an experiment for introducing scholars as residents in the Hospital of St. John. The canons were to take in the young scholars as *boarders* into their house, and look after their conduct and morals. The plan did not answer. It was an attempt to put new wine into old bottles. There came an explosion. Cambridge in the thirteenth century had not the *men* that Oxford had, so Oxford kept the lead. Perhaps there was some soreness. Did ecclesiastics shake their heads as they saw the walls of Balliol College rise, and learnt that there was just a little too much

importance given to mere scholarship, and no prominence given to theology in those early statutes of
1282? Did they, without knowing why, anticipate
with anxiety the awakening of a spirit of free thought
and free inquiry among those scholars of the Merton,
Rule? Did the orthodox party resort to prophecy,
which is seldom very complimentary or cheerful in
its utterances?

This is certain, that while Balliol College was
building there was a stir among the Benedictines,
and an effort made to assert themselves and take
their place among the learned. John Giffard started
his great college for the reception of student monks
at Oxford. It became, and for centuries continued
to be, the resort of the Benedictine order, and was
supported by levies from a large number of the old
monasteries. The inference is forced upon us that
the English monasteries no longer stood in the front
rank as seats of learning. Students and scholars
would no longer go to the monks; the monks must
go to the scholars. But the establishment of a
seminary for the reception of young monks at
Oxford tended to the strengthening of the ecclesiastical influence in that University. Cambridge lost
in the same proportion that Oxford gained. Even
the great Priory of Norwich sent its promising
young monks to Oxford, passing by the nearer and

more conveniently situated University. As early as 1288 we find entries in the Norwich Priory Rolls of payments for the support of the schools and scholars at Oxford. It was long after this that Cambridge offered any similar attraction to the " religious."

Be it noted that until Merton's day people had never heard of what we now understand by a *college*. It was a novelty in English institutions. Men and women had lived commonly enough in societies that were essentially religious in their character. Some of those societies, and only some, had drifted into becoming the quiet homes of learning as well as of devotion ; but the main business—the *raison d'être* of monks and nuns and canons—was the practice of asceticism, the keeping up of unceasing worship in the church of the monastery—the endeavour ᵗo be holier than men of the world need be, or the endeavour to make the men of the world holier than they cared to be. The religious orders were religious or they were nothing. Each new rule for the reformation of those orders aimed at restoring the primitive idea of self-immolation at the altar—a severer ritual, harder living, longer praying. Nay ! the new rules, in not a few instances, were actually aimed against learning and culture. The Merton Rule was a bringer in of new things. Merton would not call his society of scholars a *convent*, as the old monkish corporations had been designated. That sounded too much as though the mere promotion of pietism was his aim; he revived the old classical word *collegium*. There had been *collegia* at Rome before the imperial times; though some of them had been religious bodies, some were decidedly not so. They were societies which held property, pursued certain avocations, and acted in a corporate capacity for very mundane objects. Why should not there be a *collegium* of scholars? Why should students and men of learning be expected to be holier than other people? When Merton started his college at Oxford, he made it plain by his statutes that he did not intend to found a society after the old conventual type, but to enter upon a new departure.

The scholars of the new college were to take no vows; they were not to be worried with everlasting ritual observances. Special chaplains, who were presumably not expected to be scholars and students, were appointed for the ministration of the ceremonial in the church. Luxury was guarded against; poverty was not enjoined. As long as a scholar was pursuing his studies *bonâ fide*, he might remain a member of the college; if he was tired of books and bookish people, he might go.

When a man strikes out a new idea, he is not allowed to keep it to himself very long. The new

K

idea soon gets taken up; sometimes it gets improved upon; sometimes very much the reverse. For a wise man acts upon a hint, and it germinates; a fool only half apprehends the meaning of a hint, and he displays his folly in producing a caricature. Hugh de Balsham seems to have aimed at improving upon Merton's original idea. He meant well, doubtless; but his college of Peterhouse, the first college in Cambridge, was a very poor copy of the Oxford foundation. Merton was a man of genius, a man of ideas; Balsham was a man of the cloister. Moreover, he was by no means so rich as his predecessor, and he did not live to carry out his scheme. The funds were insufficient. The first college at Cambridge was long in building. Cambridge, in fact, was very unfortunate. Somehow there was none of the dash and enthusiasm, none of the passion for progress, which characterized Oxford. Cambridge had no moral genius like Grosseteste to impress his strong personality upon the movement which the friars stirred, no commanding intellect like that of Roger Bacon to attract and dazzle and lead into quite new regions of thought the ardent and eager spirits who felt that a new era had begun; no Occam or Duns Scotus or Bradwardine; no John Wiclif to kindle a new flame—say, rather, to take up the torch which had dropped from Bradwardine's hand, and continue the race which the others had run so well. What a grand succession of men it was!

Five colleges had been founded at Oxford before a second arose at Cambridge. After that they followed in rapid succession, and the reign of Edward the Third had not come to an end when no fewer than seven colleges had been opened at Cambridge. Five of them have survived to our own days, and two were eventually absorbed by the larger foundation which Henry the Seventh was ambitious of raising, and which now stands forth in its grandeur, the most magnificent educational corporation in the world.

. . . . . .

Where did all the money come from, not only to raise the original buildings in which the *University*, as a teaching body, pursued its work, but which also provided the *houses* in which the *colleges* of scholars lived and laboured?

Unhappily, we know very little of the University buildings during this early period. All the industry of Mr. Clark has not availed to penetrate the thick obscurity; but this at least is pretty certain, namely, that the earliest University buildings at Cambridge were very humble structures clustering round about the area now covered by the University schools and library, that it was not till the middle of the fourteenth century that any attempt was made to erect a building of any pretension, and that the "Schools Quadrangle was not completed till 130 years after the first stone was laid." The University of Cambridge was for ages a very poor corporation; it had no funds out of which to build halls or schools or library. The ceremonies at *commencement* and or other great occasions took place in the churches sometimes of the Augustinian, sometimes of the Franciscan friars. In these early times the gownsmen dared not contemplate the erection of a senate-house wherein to hold their meetings. When the fourteenth-century schools were planned their erection was doubtless regarded as a very bold and ambitious experiment. The money came in very slowly, the work stopped more than once, and when it proceeded it was only by public subscription that the funds were gathered. In 1466, William Wilflete, Master of Clare Hall and Chancellor of the University, actually made a journey to London to gather funds from whatever quarters he could, and he dunned his friends, and those on whom the University had any claim, so successfully that on June 25 of that year a contract for proceeding with the work was drawn up and signed, but it was nearly nine years after this before the schools were finally completed, together with a new library over them, by the special munificence of Archbishop Rotherham, who had further enriched the library with numerous volumes of great value.

The tie which bound the members of the *University* together was much weaker than that which united the members of the same *college*. The colleges were, in almost every case, founded by private munificence, and in most cases were commenced during the lifetime of the several founders ; but when we come to look into the sources of the college revenues we find that the actual gifts of money, or indeed of lands, was less than at first sight appears. A very large proportion of the endowments of these early colleges came from the *spoliation of the parochial clergy*. Popular writers in our own time declaim against the horrible sin of buying and selling church preferment, as if it were a modern abomination. Let a man only spend half an hour in examining the *fines* or records of transfers of property in England during the fourteenth century and he will be somewhat surprised to discover what a part the buying and selling of advowsons played in the business transactions of our forefathers five centuries ago. Advowsons were always in the market, and always good investments in those days. But not only so. A pious founder could do a great deal in the way of making perpetual provision for the mention of his name by posterity at a small cost if he took care to manipulate ecclesiastical property with prudence. There was a crafty device whereby the owner of the advowson could *appropriate* the tithes of a benefice to the support of any corporation which might be considered a *religious* foundation. The old monasteries had benefited to some extent from this disendowment of the secular clergy, the Augustinian canons, during the twelfth century, being the chief gainers by the pillage. When the rage for founding colleges came in, and the awful ravages of the Black Death had depopulated whole districts, the fashion of alienating the revenues of the country parsons and diverting them into the new channel grew to be quite a rage. The colleges of secular priests living together in common, or what it is now the fashion to call a clergy house, might be and were strictly *religious* foundations; and could the colleges of scholars, of teachers and learners who presumably were all priests, or intended for the priesthood, be regarded as less *religious* than the others? So it came to pass that the tithes of parish after parish were diverted into a new channel, and these very colleges at Cambridge which were professedly meant to raise the standard of education among the seculars were endowed at the expense of those same secular clergy. In order that the country

parsons might be better educated, it was arranged
that the country parsons should be impoverished!

.   .   .   .   .   .

Seven new colleges opened in less than thirty
years at Cambridge alone! Think what this must
have meant. I suspect that Oxford had attracted
the reading men, and Cambridge possessed charms
for the fast ones. How else are we to explain Archbishop Stratford's stringent order in 1342 for the
repression of the dandyism that prevailed among the
young scholars? These young Cantabs of the fourteenth century were exquisites of the first water.
Their fur-trimmed cloaks and their tippets; their
shoes of all the colours of the rainbow; their dainty
girdles, bejewelled and gilt, were a sight to see.
And then their hair! positively curled and powdered,
and growing over their shoulders, too; and when
they passed their fingers through the curls, look you,
there were rings on their fingers! Call you these
scholars? Chaucer's "Clerk of Oxenforde" was of
a very different type:—

> For all that he might of his frendes hente
> On books and in learning he it spente.

Nevertheless it can hardly have been but that the
foundation of so many colleges at Cambridge brought
in a stricter discipline; the new collegiate life of the

scholars began.   Perhaps for the majority of readers
no part of Mr. Clark's great work will prove so
attractive as the last four hundred pages, with their
delightful essays on " The Component Parts of a
College."   Here we have traced out for us in the
most elaborate manner, the gradual development of
the collegiate idea, from the time when it expressed
itself in a building that had no particular plan, down
to our own days, when colleges vie with one another
in architectural splendour and in the lavish complete-
ness of their arrangements.

At the outset the uninitiated must prepare to
have some of their favourite theories rudely shat-
tered.   We are in the habit of assuming that a
quadrangle is one of the essential features of a
college.   It is almost amazing to learn that the quad-
rangular arrangement was adopted very gradually.

Again, we are often assured that the colleges at
the two older universities are the only relics of the
monastic system, and are themselves monastic in
their origin.   A greater fallacy could hardly be pro-
pounded.   It would be nearer the truth to say that
the founding of the colleges was at once a protest
against the monasteries and an attempt to supersede
them.

More startling still is the fact that a college did
not at first necessarily imply that there was a chapel

attached. So far from this being the case, it is certain that Peterhouse, the oldest college in Cambridge, never had a chapel till the present building was consecrated in 1632. It was with great difficulty that the Countess of Pembroke in 1366 was allowed to build a chapel within the precincts of her new college; and, so far from these convenient adjuncts to a collegiate establishment having been considered an essential in early times, no less than eight of the college chapels at Cambridge and four at Oxford date from a time after the Reformation. In the fourteenth century and later the young scholars, as a rule, attended their parish church. Sometimes the college added on an aisle for the accommodation of its members; sometimes it obtained a *licence* to use a room in which Divine Service might be conducted for a time; once the founder of a college erected a collegiate quire in the middle of the parish church, a kind of gigantic *pew*, for the accommodation of his scholars. Downing College has never had a chapel to the present hour.

Of all the developments, however, in the college idea, none has been more remarkable than that of the master's lodge. In the fourteenth century the master of a college was but *primus inter pares*, and the distance between him and his *fellows* or *scholars* was less than that which exists now between the commanding officer of a regiment in barracks and his brother officers. The master had no sinecure; the discipline of the place depended upon him almost entirely, for in those days the monarchial idea was in the ascendant; the king was a real king, the bishop a real bishop, the master a real master. Everything was referred to him, everything originated with him, everything was controlled by him. But as for the accommodation assigned to him in the early colleges, it was very inferior indeed to that which every graduate at Trinity or St. John's expects to find in our time. The Provost of Oriel in 1329 was permitted by the statutes to dine apart if he pleased, and to reside outside the precincts of the college if he chose to provide for himself another residence; but this was clearly an exceptional case, for the master was at this time the actual founder of the college, and Adam de Brune might be presumed to know what was good for his successors in the office for which he himself had made provision. But for generations the master enjoyed no more than a couple of *chambers* at the most, and it was not till the sixteenth century that an official residence was provided, and then such residence consisted only of *lodgings* a little more spacious and convenient than those of any of the fellows, and in no case separated from the main buildings of the college. Even when masters of colleges began to marry (and the earliest instance of this seems to have been Dr. Heynes, Master of Queens' College, in 1529), it was long before the master's wife was so far recognized as to be received within the precincts; and as late as 1576, when the fellows of King's complained of their provost's wife being seen within the college, Dr. Goad replied that she had not been twice in the college "Quad" in her life, as far as he knew. When the great break-up came in the next century, then the establishment of the master demanded increased accommodation for his family, and the master's lodge began to grow slowly, until university architects of the nineteenth century displayed their exalted sense of what was due to the dignity of a "head of a house" by erecting two such palaces as the lodges of Pembroke and St. John's Colleges; for the glorification of the artist, it may be, but whether for the advantage of the college, the university, or the occupants of the aforesaid lodges may be reasonably doubted. One master's lodge in Cambridge *is at this moment let*, presumably for the benefit of the head of the house, whose official residence it is; and, if things go on as they are tending, the day may come —who knows how soon?—when Cambridge shall at last be able to boast of a really good hotel, "in a central and very desirable situation, commanding a delightful view of "—what shall we say?—" fitted up with every convenience, and formerly known as the Master's Lodge of St. Boniface College."

I am inclined to think that there is such a thing as architecture run to seed.

. . . . . .

If any one imagines that it would be possible within the limits of a single essay to follow Mr. Clark through the exhaustive processes of investigation which he has pursued, or to summarize at all satisfactorily the results which he has arrived at and set forth in so masterly a manner, let such an one spend only a single hour in turning over the leaves of these splendid volumes. The exquisite illustrations alone (which count by hundreds), and the elaborate maps and ground-plans, are full of surprises; they speak with an eloquence of their own to such as have eyes to see and in whom there is a spark of imagination to enlighten the paths along which their accomplished guide can lead them. Do you think that such a work as this tells us no more than how the stone walls rose and the buildings assumed their present form, and court was added to court, and libraries and museums and lecture-rooms and all the rest of them were constructed by the professional gentlemen who drew the plans, and piled up by the masons and the bricklayers ? Then you will do it a grievous injustice.

> Horizons rich with trembling spires
> On violet twilights, lose their fires

if there be no human element to cast a living glow upon them. The authors of this architectural history knew better than any one else that they were dealing with the architectural history of a great national institution. They knew that these walls—some so old and crumbling, some so new and hard and un-lovely—bear upon them the marks of all the changes and all the progress, the conflicts and the questionings, the birth-throes of the new childhood, the fading out of a perplexed senility, the earnest grappling with error, the painful searching after truth which the spirit of man has gone through in these homes of intellectual activity during the lapse of six hundred years. Do you wish to understand the buildings ? Then you must study the life ; and the converse is true also. Either explains, and is the indispensable interpreter of, the obscurities of the other. Mr. Clark could not have produced this exhaustive history of university and collegiate fabrics if he had not gained a profound insight into the student life of Cambridge from the earliest times.

How did they live, these young scholars in the early days ? Through what whimsical vagaries have the fashions changed? As the centuries have rolled on, have the youth of England become better or wiser than their sires? Neither better nor wiser seems to be the answer. The outer man is not as he was; the real moral and intellectual stamina of Englishmen has at least suffered no deterioration. Our habits are different; our dress, our language, the look of our homes, are all other than they were. Our wants have multiplied immensely; the amount of physical discomfort and downright suffering which our ancestors were called upon to endure doubtless sent up the death-rate to a figure which to us would be appalling. We start from a standing-point in moral, social, and intellectual convictions so far in advance of that of our forefathers that they could not conceive of such a *terminus ad quem* as serves us as a *terminus a quo*. In other words, we *begin* at a point in the line which they never conceived could be reached. Yet the more closely we look into the past the more do we see how history in all essentials is for ever repeating herself—impossible though it may be to put the clock back for ourselves.

How significant is the fact that through all these centuries of building and planting, of pulling down and raising up, the makers of Cambridge—that is, the men who achieved for her her place in the realms of thought, inquiry, and discovery—never seemed to have thought that Death could play much havoc among them. In the old monasteries there was always a cemetery. The canon or the monk who passed into the cloister came there once for all—to live *and die* within the walls of his monastery. The scholar who came to get all the learning he could, and who settled in some humble hostel or some unpretentious college of the old type, came to spend some few years there, but no more. He came to live his life, and when there was no more life in him—no more youthful force, activity, and enthusiasm—there was no place for him at Cambridge. There they wanted men of vigour and energy, not past their work. Die? No! as long as he was verily alive it was well that he should stay and toil. When he was a dying man, better he should go. No college at Cambridge had a cemetery. Let the dead bury their dead!

Indeed, it must have been hard for the weak and sickly—the lad of feeble frame and delicate organization—to stand that rugged old Cambridge life. "College rooms" in our time suggest something like the *ne plus ultra* of æsthetic elegance and luxury. We find it hard to realize the fact that for centuries a Fellow of a college was expected to have two or three *chamber fellows* who shared his bedroom with him; and that his *study* was no bigger than a study at the schoolhouse at Rugby, and very much smaller than a

fourth-form boy enjoys at many a more modern public
school. At the hostels, which were of course much
more crowded than the colleges were, a separate bed
was the privilege of the few. What must have been
the condition of those semi-licensed receptacles for the
poorer students in the early times, when we find as
late as 1598 that in St. John's College there were no
less than seventy members of the college " accom-
modated " (!) in twenty-eight chambers. This was
before the second court at St. John's was even begun,
and yet these seventy Johnians were living in luxury
when compared with their predecessors of two hundred years before.

" In the early colleges the windows of the chambers
were unglazed and closed with wooden shutters ;
their floors were either of clay or tiled ; and their
halls and ceilings were unplastered." We have express
testimony that at Corpus Christi College not even the
master's lodge had been glazed and panelled before
the beginning of the sixteenth century. By an inventory which Mr. Clark has printed, dated July 3,
1451, it appears that in the master's lodge at King's
College, " the wealthiest lodge of the university,
there was then only one chair ; that the tables were
supported on trestles ; and that those who used them
sat on forms or stools." As for the chambers and
studies, not only were they destitute of anything in

the shape of stoves or fire-places, but their walls were absolutely bare, while in the upper chambers there were not even lath and plaster between the tiles and the beams of the roof. It is to us almost incomprehensible how vitality could have been kept up in the winter under such conditions. The cold must have been dreadful.

At four only of five earlier and smaller colleges was there any fire-place in the hall, and the barbaric braziers in which first charcoal and afterwards coke was burned, were actually the only heating apparatus known in the immense halls of Trinity and St. John's till within the last twenty years! The magnificent hall of Trinity actually retained till 1866 the brazier *which had been in use for upwards of* 160 *years!* The clumsy attempt to fight the bitter cold which was usual in our mediæval churches and manor-houses, by strewing the stone floor with rushes, was carried out too in the college halls, and latterly, instead of rushes, sawdust was used, at least in Trinity. "It was laid on the floor at the beginning of winter, and turned over with a rake as often as the upper surface became dirty. Finally, when warm weather set in, it was removed, the colour of charcoal!" Well might the late Professor Sedgwick, in commenting upon this practice, exclaim: "The dirt was sublime in former years!"

Yet in the earliest times a lavatory was provided in the college halls, and a towel of eight or nine yards long, which at Trinity, as late as 1612, was hung on a hook—the refinement of hanging a towel on a *roller* does not appear to have been thought of. These towels were for use *before* dinner ; *at* dinner the fellows of Christ's in 1575 were provided with table-napkins. If they wiped their fingers on the table-cloth they were fined a penny. The temptation must have been strong at times, for *no forks were in use*—not even the iron-pronged forks which some of us remember in hall in our young days. The oldest piece of furniture in the college halls were the stocks, set up for the correction of refractory undergraduates who should have been guilty of the enormity of bathing in the Cam or other grave offence and scandal.

Of the amusements indulged in by the undergraduates at Cambridge in the early times we hear but little. The probability seems to be that they had to manage for themselves as best they could. Gradually the bowling-green, the butts for archery, and the tennis-courts were provided by several colleges. Tennis seems to have been the rage at Cambridge during the sixteenth century, and the tennis-courts became sources of revenue in the Elizabethan time, It is clear that by this time the old severity and rigour had become relaxed, the colleges had become richer, and in another hundred years the combination-rooms had become comfortable and almost luxurious before the seventeeth century closed. In Queens' College in 1693 there were actually *flowers* in the combination-room, and at Christ's College in 1716 a card-table was provided " in the fellows' parlour."

．　　．　　．　　．　　．　　．

It may be said that the immense expansion of the University, as distinct from a mere aggregate of colleges, dates from the beginning of the eighteenth century. Up to that time the colleges had for four hundred years been steadily growing into privileged corporations, whose wealth and power had been too great for the Commonwealth, of which they were in idea only members. With the Georgian era the new movement began. When Bishop Moore's vast library was presented by George II. to the *University*, when the first stone of the Senate House was laid in 1722, when the *University* arranged for the reception of Dr. Woodward's fossils in 1735—these events marked the beginning of a new order of things. Whatever confusion may have existed in the minds of our grandfathers, who had a vague conviction that the University meant no more than the aggregate of the colleges, and a suspicion that what the University was the colleges made it—we, in our generation, have been assured that the colleges owed their existence to the sufferance of universities; or, if that be putting the case too strongly, that the colleges exist for the sake of the University. The new view has at any rate gained the approval of the Legislature; the University is in no danger of being predominated over by the colleges in the immediate future; the danger rather is lest the colleges should be starved or at least impoverished for the glorification of the University, the college-fellowships being shorn of their dignity and emoluments in order to ensure that the University officials shall become the exclusive holders of the richest prizes.

For good or evil we have entered upon a new career. The old Cambridge, which some of us knew in our youth, with its solemn ecclesiasticism, its quaint archaisms, its fantastic anomalies, its fascinating picturesqueness, its dear old barbaric unintelligible odds and ends that met us at every turn in street and chapel and hall—that old Cambridge is as dead as the Egypt of the Pharaohs. The new Cambridge, with its bustling syndics for ever on the move—its bewildering complexity of examinations—its " sweet girl-graduates with their golden hair," its delightful " notion of grand and capacious and massive amusement," its glorious wealth of collections and appliances and facilities for every kind of study and research, is alive with an exuberant vitality.

What form will the new life assume in the time that is coming ? Will the Cambridge of six centuries hence be able to produce such a record of her past as that which she can boast of now ? Among her *alumni* of the future will there arise again any such loyal and enlightened historians as these who have raised to themselves and their University so noble a monument ?

VII.

THE PROPHET OF WALNUT-TREE YARD.

"Did you ever hear tell of Lodowick Muggleton?"

"Not I."

"That is strange. Know then that he was the founder of our poor society, and after him we are frequently, though opprobriously, termed Muggletonians, for we are Christians. Here is his book; I will sell it cheap."—LAVENGRO.

SCRUPULOUS veracity was hardly a characteristic of the late George Borrow. A man of great memory, he was also a man of fertile imagination, and where the two are found in excess, side by side in the same intellect, they are apt to twine round one another, so to speak, and the product is something which the matter-of-fact man abhors. I do not doubt that Borrow did meet a Muggletonian at Bristol—I think it was there—some sixty years ago; but I am pretty sure that he knew very little indeed about the Muggletonians, and that he could have hardly opened the

book which he implies that he purchased, and which
I am almost certain he never read. I have a strong
suspicion that he very much antedated the incident
which he narrates, for I myself knew an old second-
hand bookseller in a back street at Bristol, who was
a Muggletonian, with whom I made acquaintance
when a lad. He was a slow-speaking, wary,
suspicious, and dirty old man, and as I had not
sufficient funds to be a good customer, I daresay he
did not think it worth his while to be communicative,
but he told me one day that he had been one of the
original subscribers to the *Spiritual Epistles* which
were reprinted in quarto years before I was born;
though, as he confessed, his name does not appear
on the list of names printed at the end of the preface,
which list, he assured me, was very incomplete, as
he from his own knowledge could certify. This old
man would have been very old indeed if he had been
old when Borrow was a youth; and yet, as I say, I
suspect he was the very man of whom mention is
made in the extract I have given above. He was
the only Muggletonian I ever knew, but he certainly
was not the last of his sect, and I should not be at
all surprised to hear that it is a flourishing sect still,
and that it still has its assemblies, its votaries, its
literature, and its propaganda. It is true that the
name *Muggletonians* does not appear in that astonish-

ing list of religious denominations which the Regis-trar-General was enabled to compile for the year 1883; but that proves little, inasmuch as the closer a religious corporation is, the more exclusive, the less does it care to register the name of the building in which it may choose to assemble for worship; and I observe that the Southcotians are no longer to be found upon that list, though I happen to know that they are not extinct yet, nor has their faith in their prophetess and her mission quite died out from the face of the earth.

This is certain, that as late as 1820 an edition of the *Spiritual Epistles*, which must have cost at that time two or three hundred pounds to print, was subscribed for, and that nine years afterwards ap-peared *Divine Songs of the Muggletonians*—they were not ashamed of the name—printed also by subscrip-tion, filling 621 pages, and showing pretty clearly that there had of late been a strange revival of the sect: an outburst of new fervour having somehow been awakened, and an irrepressible passion for writing "Songs" having displayed itself, which had not been without its effect in resuscitating dormant enthusiasm. The vagaries of the human mind in what, for want of any better designation, we call "religious belief" have always had for me a peculiar fascination, as they have for others. Epiphanius.

whose name is and used to be a terror to her Royal Highness in days gone by, when I insisted upon reading to her about the peculiar people who made it a matter of faith to eat bread and cheese at the Eucharist—Epiphanius is to me positively entertaining, and Pagitt's *Heresiography* is none the less instructive because it is a vulgar catch-penny little book, made up, like Peter Pindar's razors, to sell. To me it seems that to dismiss even the wildest and foolishest opinion *which makes way*, as if it were a mere absurdity that does not deserve notice, is to show a certain flippancy and shallowness. Do not all thoughtful men pass through certain stages of intellectual growth, and are not the convictions of our youth held very differently from those which we find ourselves swayed by in our later years? The beliefs which the multitude take up with are such as the untrained and the half-trained are always captivated by, whether individually or in the mass. There are limits to our powers of assimilation according as our development has been arrested or is still going on, and he who hopes to understand the course of human affairs or to make any intelligent forecast of what is coming can never afford to neglect the study of morbid appetites or morbid anatomy in the domain of mind.

There is a strong family likeness among all fanatics; and this is characteristic of them all, that they are profusely communicative and absolutely honest. Prophets have no secrets, no reserve, no doubts, they are always true men. John Reeve and Lodowick Muggleton are no exception to the general rule. We can follow their movements pretty closely for some years. The book of *The Acts of the Witnesses of the Spirit* furnishes us with quite as much as we want to know about the sayings and doings of the grotesque pair and their early extravagances; and Muggleton's letters cover a period of forty years, during all which time he was going in and out among the artisans and small traders of the city, obstinately asserting himself in season and out of season, and leaving behind him in his eccentric chronicle such a minute and faithful picture of London life among the middle—the lower middle—class during the last half of the seventeenth century as is to be found nowhere else. The reader must be prepared for the most startling freaks of language, for very vulgar profanity, the more amazing because so manifestly unintended. When people break away from all the traditions of the past and surrender themselves to absolute anarchy in morals and religion the old terminology ceases to be employed in the old way, ceases indeed to have any meaning. The prophet or the philosopher who sets himself to invent a new theory of the universe or a new creed

for his followers to embrace, can hardly avoid shocking and horrifying those who are content to use
words as their forefathers did and attach to these
words the same sort of sacredness that the Hebrews
did to the Divine name. There is no need to do
more than allude to this side of the Muggletonian
writing. What we are concerned with is the story
of the prophet's life, which has been told with the
utmost frankness and simplicity; a more unvar-
nished tale it would be difficult to find, or one which
bears more the stamp of truth upon its every line.

The Acts of the Witnesses of the Spirit is a posthu-
mous work written by Muggleton when he was very
old, and left behind him in manuscript with direc-
tions that it should be published after his death. It
is a quarto volume of 180 pages and is a book of
some rarity. It was published in 1699, with an
epistle dedicatory to all true Christian people, apparently written by Thomas Tomkinson, one of the
chosen seed. After preparing us for what is coming
by dwelling upon the wonderful stories in the Old
Testament and the New, Muggleton plunges into his
subject by giving us a brief account of his own and
his brother prophet's parentage and early biography.
Let the reader understand that here beginneth the
third chapter of *The Acts of the Witnesses* at the third
verse :—

"3. As for John Reeve, he was born in Wiltshire; his father was clerk to a deputy of Ireland, a gentleman as we call them by his place, but fell to decay.

"4. So he put John Reeve apprentice here at London to a tailor by trade. He was out of his apprenticeship before I came acquainted with him; he was of an honest, just nature, and harmless.

"5. But a man of no great natural wit or wisdom; no subtlety or policy was in him, nor no great store of religion; he had lost what was traditional; only of an innocent life.

"7. And I, Lodowick Muggleton, was born in Bishop-gate Street, near the Earl of Devonshire's house, at the corner house called Walnut-tree Yard.

"8. My father's name was John Muggleton; he was a smith by trade—that is, a farrier or horse doctor; he was in great respect with the postmaster in King James's time; he had three children by my mother, two sons and one daughter, I was the youngest and my mother loved me."

His mother died, his father married again, whereupon the boy was sent into the country—*boarded out* as we say—and kept there till his sixteenth year, when he was brought back to London and apprenticed to a tailor—one John Quick—"a quiet, peaceable man, not cruel to servants, which liked me very well." Muggleton took to his trade and pleased his master. The journeymen were a loose lot, "bad husbands and given to drunkenness, but my nature was inclined to be sober." Hitherto the young man had received no religious training; when he had served his time, however, "hearing in those days great talk among the vulgar people and especially amongst youth, boys, and young maids, of a people called Puritans. . . . I liked their discourse upon the Scriptures and pleaded for a holy keeping of the Sabbath day, which my master did not do, nor I his servant."

This must have been about the year 1630—for Muggleton was born in June 1610—when the Sabbatarian controversy was at its height, and the feeling of the country was approaching fever heat, and when Charles the First had resolved to try and govern without a Parliament, and when Archbishop Abbot was in disgrace, and Laud had begun to exercise his predominant influence. Muggleton was but little impressed by "the people called Puritans," and he went on his old way. When he had nearly served his time, he began to look about him. The tailor's trade did not seem likely to lead to much, unless it were combined with something else, and a brilliant opening offered itself, as he was at work for a pawn-broker in Hounsditch. "The broker's wife had one daughter alive. The mother, being well persuaded of my good natural temper, and of my good husbandry, and that I had no poor kindred come after me to be any charge or burthen to her daughter, . . . proposed to me that she would give me a hundred pounds with her to set up. . . . So the maid and I were made sure by promise, and I was resolved to have the maid to wife, and to keep a broker's shop, and lend money on pawns, and grow rich as others did." Muggleton had not yet been admitted to the freedom of the city, and the marriage was arranged to take place after he should have done so. In the meantime he found himself working side by side with William Reeve, Prophet John Reeve's brother, at this time a "very zealous Puritan," with whom he talked of his prospects. "I loved the maid, and desired to be rich," he tells us; but these Puritan people were horrified at his deliberately intending to live the life of a usurer, and they "threatened great judgments, and danger of damnation hereafter."

It is clear that the frightful eschatology of the time was exercising a far greater power upon the imagination of the masses than anything else. People were dwelling upon all that was terrible and gloomy in the picture of a future life; the one thought with the visionaries was this—Save yourselves from the wrath to come. " I was extremely fearful of eternal damnation," says Muggleton, "thinking my soul might go into hell fire without a body, as all people did at that time."

There was evidently a struggle between conviction and inclination, and it ended as we should have expected—the marriage was broken off. Then followed some years of vehement religious conflict; "Neither did I hear any preach in these days but the Puritan ministers, whose hair was cut short. *For if a man with long hair had gone* into the pulpit to preach, I would have gone out of the Church again, though he might preach better than the other." All through this time visions of hell and torment, and devils and damnation troubled him; now and then there were "elevations in my mind, but these were few and far between; a while after all was lost again." He soon consoled himself for his matrimonial disappointment; he married and had three daughters, then his first wife died. He throve in his calling, "only the spirit of fear of hell was still upon me, but not so extreme as it was before." He took a second wife, and the civil war began.

"And generally the Puritans were all for the Parliament, and most of my society and acquaintance did fall away and declined in love one towards another. Some of them turned to Presbytery, and some turned Independents; others fell to be Ranters, and some fell to be mere Atheists. So that our Puritan people were so divided and scattered in our religion, that I was altogether at a loss; for all the zeal we formerly had was quite worn out. For I had seen the utmost perfection and satisfaction that could be found in that way, except I would do it for loaves, *but loaves was never my aim.*"

The civil war ran its course, but Muggleton cared nothing for the general course of events. What were kings and bishops and Lords and Commons to him? he was living in quite another world. As for Laud and Strafford, and Pym and Hampden, he does not even once name them. He makes not the slightest allusion to the death of Charles the First, though he was living within half a mile of Whitehall when the king's head fell on the block. Prophets of the Muggleton type are so busied about their own souls and their own spiritual condition, that the battles, murders, and sudden deaths of other men, great or small, give them no concern whatever.

A couple of years or so after the execution of the king, " it came to pass I heard of several prophets and prophetesses that were about the streets. . . . Also I heard of two other men that were counted greater than prophets—to wit, John Tannye and John Robins. John Tannye, he declared himself to be the Lord's High Priest, therefore he circumcised himself according to the law. Also he declared that he was to gather the Jews out of all nations, . . . with many other strange and wonderful things. And as for John Robins, he declared himself to be God Almighty. Also he said that he had raised from the dead several of the prophets, as Jeremiah and others. Also I saw several others of the prophets that was said to be raised by him, *for I have had nine or ten of them at my house at a time, of those that were said to be raised from the dead.*"

Is madness contagious? Or is it that, while the sane can exercise but a very limited power over the insane, there is no limit to the influence which the insane can gain over one another? Living in a world of their own, where delusions pass for palpable facts, where the logical faculty accepts the wildest visions as of equal significance with actual realities, these dreamers have a calculus of their own which includes the symbols in use among the sane, but comprehends besides a notation which these latter attach no meaning to, reject, and deride.

"Would you be so kind as tell me, sir, what's a ohm?" said the worthy Mr. Stiggins to me the other day. "It's a modern term used in electricity, which I am too ignorant to explain to you." He looked full at me for more than five seconds without a word then he said, "I'm thinking that this man

L

was a fool to talk about ohms when not even you
knew what a ohm means. And he came from
Cambridge College too, and he's got a vote! I
reckon when a man can't talk the same as other
folks he'd ought to be shut up." Indignant Stiggins!
But are we not all intolerant?

John Robins had acquired an almost unlimited
ascendency over his crazy prophets, and speedily
acquired the like ascendency over Muggleton. What
specially fascinated him was that all John Robins's
prophets "had power from him to damn any that did
oppose or speak evil of him. So his prophets gave
sentence of damnation upon many, to my knowledge,
for speaking evil of him, they not knowing him
whether he was true or false." Muggleton was
profoundly impressed, but according to his own
account he was a silent observer, and waited. One
of the prophets often came to his house and was
welcome; he "spake as an angel of God, and I never
let him go without eating and drinking," for Muggleton was a man of large appetite and demanded large
supplies of food, nor did he stint himself of meat
and drink or withhold creature comforts from those
he loved.

Just at this time Muggleton "fell into a melan-
choly." He had arrived at the prophetic age; he

had completed his fortieth year. " Then did two motives arise in me and speak in me as two lively voices, as if two spirits had been speaking in me, one answering the other as if they were not my own spirit." So that our noble laureate was anticipated by two centuries, unless indeed the "two lively voices" make themselves heard at times to most men who have ears to hear them. Muggleton's voices were not very high-toned voices; they were voices that spake of heaven and hell, nothing more. Love and duty never seem to have formed the subject of his meditations. "For I did not so much mind to be saved, as I did to escape being damn'd. For I thought, if I could but lie still in the earth for ever, it would be as well with me as it would be if I were in eternal happiness . . . for I did not care whether I was happy so I might not be miserable. I cared not for heaven so I might not go to hell. These things pressed hard upon my soul, even to the wounding of it."

The battle within him went on fiercely for some time, and it ended as we should have expected. " I was so well satisfied in my mind as to my eternal happiness, that I was resolved now to be quiet and to get as good a living as I could in this world and live as comfortably as I could here, thinking that this revelation should have been beneficial to nobody but myself." The "motional voices," and visions, and questionings, continued from April 1651 to January 1652 ; and it was during this time that the intimacy between Muggleton and Reeve became more closely cemented, for " John Reeve was so taken with my language that his desires were *extreme earnest* that he might have the same revelation as I had. His desires were so great that he was trouble-some unto me, for if I went into one room, into another, he would follow me to talk to me." His persistence was rewarded, and just when Muggleton's visions ceased " in the month of January 1652, about the middle of the month, John Reeve came to me very joyful and said, Cousin Lodowick, now said he, I know what revelation of Scripture is as well as thee." Reeve's revelations increased, and never ceased for two weeks. " First visions, then by voice of words to the hearing of the ear three mornings together the third, fourth, and fifth days of February 1652, and the year of John Reeve's life forty-two, and the year of my life forty-one."

Two men in this curious ecstatic condition obviously could not stop at this point. It was a critical moment—would they enter into rivalry or spiritual partnership ? If the latter, then who was to be the leader, who would make the first move ? It was soon settled.

" The first evening God *spake* to John Reeve he came to my house and said, Cousin Lodowick, God hath given thee unto me for ever, and the tears ran down both sides his cheeks amain. So I asked him what was the matter, for he looked like one that had been risen out of the grave, he being a fresh-coloured man the day before, but the tears ran down his cheeks apace." John Reeve was not yet prepared to deliver his commission with authority ; it was coming, but not yet. Meanwhile he turned to Muggleton's children and pronounced them blessed, " but especially thy daughter Sarah, she shall be the teacher of all the women in London." Sarah was hiding on the stairs and was not a little afraid ; she was a girl of fourteen, but she accepted her mission there and then.

She proved to be a valuable helper, " and several persons came afterwards to my house more to discourse with her than us, and they marvelled that one so young should have such knowledge and wisdom." Next day John Reeve came again, and Muggleton was pronounced to be the *mouth* of the new revelation, " as Aaron was given to be Moses' mouth."

The first thing to be done was to depose the other two prophets, Robins and Tannye, and to hoise them on their own petard. It had to be seen who could damn hardest. For one moment even Muggle-

ton's stout heart failed, he would take another with
him to be present at the great trial of strength. He
called upon a certain Thomas Turner to accompany
him, " else you must be cursed to all eternity. But
his wife was exceeding wroth and fearful, and she
said, if John Reeve came again to her husband that
she would run a spit in his guts, so John Reeve
cursed her to eternity." Whereupon Turner, ap-
palled by the sentence, complied with the order and
went. The three presented themselves before the
other madman, and John Reeve uttered his testimony, denouncing him as a false prophet and gave
him a month to repent of his misdeeds. When the
month had elapsed Reeve wrote the sentence of
eternal damnation upon him " and left it at his
lodging, and after a while he and his great matters
perished in the sea. For he made a little boat to
carry him to Jerusalem, and going to Holland to
call the Jews there, he and one Captain James was
cast away and drowned, so all his powers came to
nothing."

The day after the interview with Tannye, the
prophets proceeded to deal with John Robins. He
had been thrown into Bridewell by Cromwell, and
there he lay, his worshippers still resorting to him
for any one with money could visit a prisoner in gaol
as often as he pleased. When the prophets appeared

at the gate empty handed, the keeper as a matter of course refused them admittance. Then said John Reeve to the keeper, " Thou shall never be at peace." By and by they were shown where Robins's cell was ; they summoned him to the window, and a strange interview took place, which is minutely described. It ended by Reeve delivering his charge and pronouncing his sentence. Many had been the crimes of John Robins. He had ruined and deceived men in a multitude of ways ; among others " thou givest them leave to abstain by degrees from all kinds of food, thou didst feed them with windy things, as apples and other fruit that was windy, and they drank nothing but water ; therefore look what measure thou hast measured to others we will measure again to thee."

John Robins was utterly mastered ; " he pulled his hands off the grates and laid them together and said, It is finished ; the Lord's will be done." In two months he had written a letter of recantation, was released from durance, and is heard of no more.

" Thus the reader may see that these two powers were brought down in these two days' messages from the Lord."

The world was all before them now. It remained that the new prophets should have some distinctive dogma, and that the printing press should be called in as an accessory to spread their fame. Again John Reeve took the lead, and in 1652 he wrote an account of his divine commission and published his first work, *A Transcendant Spiritual Treatise*, which told of his last revelation of the message to Tannye and Robins.

While the book was passing through the press the prophets lived by their trade, and made no attempt to preach before any assembly. They *talked* incessantly, and they cursed liberally. At last the children in the streets began to follow Reeve and pelt him, crying after him, " There goes the prophet that damns people ! " Muggleton, meanwhile, was always ready to meet an inquirer, and to eat and drink with him. " On one occasion an old acquaintance would needs have me drink with him, that he might have some talk with me, and there followed a neighbour of his, a gentleman, as we call them ; his name was Penson, and he sat down in our company." Soon Penson began to deride and abuse the prophet ; whereupon Muggleton calmly " did pronounce this Penson cursed to eternity." Penson did not like being damned under the circumstances. " Then he rose up, and with both his fists smote upon my head. . . But it came to pass that this Penson was sick immediately after, and in a week or ten days after he died, much troubled in his mind, and tormented insomuch that his friends and relations sought to apprehend me for a witch, he being a rich man, but they couldn't tell how to state the matter, so they let it fall."

It is pretty clear that John Reeve was from the first disposed to go beyond his brother prophet; and shortly after the incident of Penson's death Reeve made a grand *coup*, which produced a profound impression. Muggleton had damned a *gentleman*. Reeve tried his power upon the same class, and succeeded in actually converting two of them, who were influential men among the Ranters. The Ranters were startled and puzzled. "And it came to pass that one of these Ranters kept a victualling house and sold drink in the Minories, and they would spend their money there. So John Reeve and myself came there, and many of them despised our declaration. So John Reeve gave sentence of eternal damnation upon many of them, and one of them, being more offended than all the rest, was moved with such wrath and fury that five or six men could hardly keep him off, his fury was so hot. Then John Reeve said unto the people standing by, 'Friends,' said he, 'I pray you stand still on both sides of the room, and let there be a space in the middle, and I will lay down my head upon the ground and let this furious man tread upon my

head and do what he will unto me. . . .' So John
Reeve pulled off his hat and laid his face flat to the
ground, and the people stood still. So the man came
running with great fury, and when he came near
him, lifting up his foot to tread on his neck, the man
started back again and said, 'No, I scorn to tread
upon a man that lieth down to me.' And the people
all marvelled at this thing."

Though Muggleton does not make much of this
incident, it appears to have been a very important
one in the early history of the sect, for from this
moment the numbers of Muggletonians began to
increase, and they began to absorb a small army of
wandering monomaniacs who were roaming about
London and talking about *religion*, and visions, and
revelations, and attaching themselves first to one
body and then to another, according as they could
get admission to the meeting-houses and be allowed
to preach and harangue. Astrologers too, came
and conferred with the prophets, and drunken
scoffers laid bets that they would get the prophet's
blessing; and on one occasion a company of
"Atheistical Ranters" made a plot to turn the
tables upon Muggleton, and damn him and Reeve.
Three of "the most desperatest" agreed to do it.
"So the time appointed came, and there was prepared a good dinner of pork, and the three came

ready prepared to curse us." Part of the agreement was that the dinner should follow upon the cursing. But whether it was that the rogues could do nothing until they were fortified with drink, or that a sudden spasm of conscientiousness came upon them, or that they were like superstitious people who with blanched lips loudly protest that they do not believe in ghosts, but decline on principle to walk through a churchyard after dark, these three fellows all ran away from their engagements at the eleventh hour. "So they departed without their dinner of pork."

The prophets were becoming notorious. The Ranters and John Robins had been vanquished; their first book was published and was selling; they were advertising themselves widely, and being advertised by friends and foes; but as yet they had not been persecuted, and as yet they had not put very prominently forward any distinctive or special theology. They claimed to be prophets, but their mission, What was it? What were they charged to proclaim?

It was just about this time that the works of Jacob Boehm had begun to exercise a very great influence upon the visionaries in England. The *Mercurius Teutonicus* was first published in an English translation in 1649, and the *Signatura*

Rerum had appeared in 1651. Muggleton had certainly read these books, and as certainly turned them to account. The jargon of the German mystic was exactly what he wanted in his present state of mind, and there was that in the new philosophy which commended itself vastly to him. Not that he, as an inspired prophet, could for one moment admit that he had received any light from man or was under any obligation to anything but the divine illumination enlightening him directly and immediately; but the obligation was there all the same, and to Jacob Boehm's influence we must attribute the evolution of the distinctive doctrine of the Muggletonians, which just about this time comes into obtrusive prominence.

It was at the beginning of the year 1653 that the prophets made their first important convert. Up to this time they had been heard of only in the back streets of London. But now a New England merchant named Leader, who had made a fortune in America, and had come back in disgust at the intolerance and persecution that prevailed among the colonists, made advances to Muggleton. Leader was in a despondent state of mind, and on the lookout for a religion with some novelty in it. He too had, it seems, been a student of Jacob Boehm, and the *Signatura Rerum* had opened out a new line of speculation to him. "His first question was concerning God—whether God, that created all things, could admit of being any form of Himself?"

Prophets are never at a nonplus, and never surprised by a question; the more transcendental the problem, the more need for the prophetic gift to solve it. In fact, the prophet comes in to help when all human cunning is at fault.

Accordingly Mr. Leader's question led to a discussion which is all set down at full for those who choose to read it, and as the result of that discussion comes out into clearness the astounding declaration which henceforth appears as the main article of the Muggletonian theology.

"God hath a body of His own, as man hath a body of his own; only God's body is spiritual and heavenly, clear as *christial*, brighter than the sun, swifter than thought, yet a body."

Hitherto the prophets had been groping after a formula which might be their strength, but they had not been able to put it into shape. Jacob Boehm's mysticism, passing through the alembic of such a mind as Leader's, and subjected to that occult atmosphere which Muggleton lived in, came forth in the shape of a new theology, transcendental, unintelligible, but therefore celestial and sublime. The prophets from this moment made a new departure.

Meanwhile, the unhesitating and authoritative damning of opponents exercised a strange fascination over the multitude. Reeve and Muggleton lived among the blackguards at their first start, and they damned the blackguards pretty freely. In numberless instances the blackguards were to all intents and purposes damned before Muggleton's sentence was pronounced. They were fellows given over to drink and debauchery, sots who had not much life in them, scoundrels who were in hiding, skulking in the vilest holes of the city, whom the plague or famine would be likely to rid the world of any day. They died frequently enough after the sentence was pronounced, and it is quite conceivable that the sentence may have hastened the end of many a poor wretch who had nothing to live for. Nay, in more cases than one a timid man, when the sentence was passed, was so terrified that he took to his bed there and then, and never rose from it, or became insane, neglected his business, and so was ruined ; and as the number of the damned was always increasing, the chances of strange accidents and misfortunes would go on increasing also. People heard of these, and of these only.

What the prophets themselves did, it was only natural that their followers would try to do also ; indeed, it is wonderful that the damning prerogative was not invaded much oftener than it was. It was very rarely intruded upon, however. Once, indeed, a misguided and too venturous believer named Cooper took upon him to usurp authority, and pronounced the sentence of damnation upon a small batch of fifteen scoffers who had jeered at him and the prophet's mission. The precedent was a dangerous one, there was no telling what it would lead to if such random and promiscuous damning was to go on. Next day Cooper fell grievously sick, and conscience smote him ; he could not be at peace till he had confessed his fault and been forgiven. He was forgiven accordingly, but he was admonished to lay to heart the warning, and to presume no more. " Not but that I do believe," says Muggleton, " they will all be damned," all the whole fifteen !

The movement was becoming a nuisance by this time, and Reeve got a hint, and no obscure one, that a warrant would be issued against him, " either from General Cromwell, or the Council of State, or from the Parliament." So far from being deterred by the prospect—was there ever a prophet who was frightened into silence ?—he declared that if Cromwell or the Parliament should despise him and his mission, " I would pronounce them damned as I do you ! " Though no warrant came from the Council or Cromwell—a matter much to be regretted—yet a

warrant was taken out by five of the opponents, and
the prophets were brought before the Lord Mayor.
As usual, a detailed account is given of the pro-
ceedings, which are valuable as illustrating the
method pursued in those days in the examination of
an accused person, and the procedure of the court—
so very different from our modern practice. The
prophets were committed for trial; they refused to
give bail, and were thrown into Newgate. It was
the 15th of September, 1653, one of the great festivals
among the believers. The hideous picture of prison
life in Newgate deserves to be read even by those
who have some acquaintance with the horrors of our
prisons at this time. The prophets were well
supplied with money, and so were spared some of
the worst sufferings of the place; but it was bad
enough, in all conscience, and one night the two
narrowly escaped being hanged in their own room
and were only saved by five condemned men, who
came to the rescue. Muggleton says the highwaymen and *the boys* were most set against him; one of
the highwaymen, whenever he saw him in the Hall,
"would come and deride at me, and say, 'You
rogue, you damn'd folks.' And so it was with the
boys that were prisoners; they would snatch off my
hat, and pawn it for half-a-dozen of drink. So the
boys did, and I gave them sixpence every time they

did it, to please them." Highly gratifying to the boys!

While the two were in Newgate John Reeve wrote a letter to the Lord Mayor and another to the Recorder, mildly damning them both. If we are to believe Muggleton, the Recorder was somewhat disturbed and alarmed by the sentence. When the day of trial came, Reeve bade the Lord Mayor hold his peace and be silent, as became a damned man in the presence of the prophets, and we are told the Mayor obeyed and said nothing more. The two were condemned, nevertheless, and thrown into Bridewell for seven months. Under the horrors of that dreadful imprisonment Reeve's constitution broke down. He was never the same man again. He languished on, indeed, for four years more, but he was a dying man, and he spent his time in writing books, his followers kindly ministering to him in his broken health and feebleness. The end came to him while visiting some convents at Maidstone—good women, of course. "The one was Mrs. Frances, the eldest; the second, Mrs. Roberts; the third, Mrs. Boner. This Mrs. Frances closed up his eyes, for he said unto her, 'Frances, close up mine eyes, lest my enemies say I died a staring prophet.'"

While Reeve and Muggleton were lying in New-

gate, another mystic—are we to call him a prophet
too?—was lying in Carlisle gaol. George Fox, the
Quaker, had fallen into the hands of Wilfrid Lawson,
then High Sheriff for the county, who had not
spared him. Just about the time that the London
prophets were discharged, Fox arrived in London
under the custody of Captain Drury, and had that
memorable interview with Cromwell which readers
of Fox's Journal are not likely to forget, though
Carlyle has gone far to spoil the story by slurring
it over.

It was a great event to the Quakers to have their
leader in London. He had only once before been in
the Metropolis—that was nine years ago—and then
he had been "fearful," had done nothing, was
tongue-tied, and had gladly escaped to itinerate
among the *steeple houses* in the north. This time
he had gained acceptance with the Protector. No
man would meddle with him from henceforth or let
them look to it! The Quakers were, of course,
elated; they were going to carry all before them;
they met to organize a grand campaign for prosely-
tizing all England. The two *commissionated prophets*
were by no means dismayed, by no means inclined
to be outdone by the Quakers; they invited them
to a disputation—a trial of the spirits, in fact. It
came off, accordingly, in Eastcheap, and George

Fox was there, and with him two or three of his "ministers whom the Lord raised up." It is not a little significant that Fox makes no mention of this meeting in his Journal—significant because he never omits to speak of his successes, and never tells us anything of his failures. Nay, he studiously omits all mention of Muggleton's name throughout the Journal, and in his books against him indulges in really violent language. Muggleton, on the other hand, speaks of this discussion at Eastcheap as if it had been a serious check to the Quakers, and from this time to his death he never ceased to assail them with a resolute aggressiveness which indicates no sort of misgiving in his power to deal with his antagonists. The discussion, however, ended in Fox and his supporters—five in all—receiving the sentence of damnation from the two prophets, and from this moment there was internecine war between the Quakers and the Muggletonians; each denouncing the other fiercely, and issuing books against the other by the score—works which have happily been long ago forgotten, to the great advantage of mankind. If, however, any one, curious in such lore, is desirous of finding out what cursing and swearing, regarded as one of the Fine Arts, may achieve when skilfully managed by adepts, let him by all means turn to the pamphlets of Pennington,

Richard Farnsworth, and others of the Quaker body, while delivering their souls against Muggleton, and the counterblasts of Muggleton, Claxton, and their friends in reply. One of the choicest diatribes of these *esprits forts*, as we may well call them, was hurled at the prophet by William Penn.

Muggleton had some very zealous converts at Cork—for there were believers everywhere by this time—and as they were people of substance and much in favour, they were making some way. Of course they came into collision with the Quakers, and not without success. Penn had early fallen under the influence of Richard Farnsworth, whom Muggleton had damned in 1654, and Penn's father had sent him over to manage his Irish estates, in the hope of getting the new notions out of the young man's head. The experiment failed, and young Penn, now only twenty-four years old, had returned to England in 1668 as staunch a Quaker as ever. There was a leading man among the Quakers, Josiah Cole by name, whom Muggleton had solemnly damned; he was in failing health, and he died a few days after the sentence was pronounced. The Muggletonians were jubilant, and some of the Quakers were disturbed and alarmed. Penn's heart was moved within him, and with all the fervid indignation of youth he stepped forward to draw the sword of the Lord. He printed a letter to Muggleton which should reassure the waverers. It thundered out defiance. "Boast not," he says, "thou enemy of God, thou son of perdition and confederate with the unclean croaking spirits reserved under chains to eternal darkness. . . . I boldly challenge thee with thy six-foot God and all the host of Luciferian spirits, with all your commissions, curses, and sentences, to touch and hurt me. And this know, O Muggleton: on you I trample, and to the bottomless pit are you sentenced, from whence you came, and where the endless worm shall gnaw and torture your imaginary soul."

Muggleton replied with his usual coolness, and pronounced his sentence upon the young enthusiast. Neither was a man easily to be put down; but whereas the prophet's followers were wholly unmoved by all the attacks upon them, the Quakers found the Muggletonians extremely troublesome, and it is impossible to resist the conviction that large numbers of the Quakers were won over to join the opposite camp. Nay, it looks as if Muggleton had really some strange power over the weaker vessels among the Quakers, and had actually *frightened* some of them. Writing in 1670, he says: "You are not like the people you were sixteen years ago; there were few Quakers then, but they had witchcraft fits, but now of late I do not hear of any Quaker that hath any fits, no, not so much as to buz and hum before the fit comes. But if you, Fox, doth know of any of you Quakers that have any of those witchcraft fits as formerly, bring them to me, and I shall cast out that devil which causeth those fits." The Quakers could hardly have been as angry as they were, nor their books have been so many and their writers so voluble during twenty years and longer, if Muggleton had not been a disputant to be dreaded, and a prophet with the faculty of drawing others after him.

In the whole course of his career, which extended over nearly half a century, Muggleton never found any difficulty in maintaining his authority over his followers. There were indeed two attempts at mutiny, but they were promptly suppressed, and they collapsed before they had made any head. The first was in 1660, shortly after the death of John Reeve. Lawrence Claxton, a "great writer" among the Muggletonians, had during Reeve's long illness come very much to the fore as an opponent of the Quakers, and his success had a little turned his head. In one passage of his writings he had taken rank as Reeve's equal and representative, and had put himself on a level with "the Commissionated." It was an awful act of impiety. "For," says

Muggleton, "as John Reeve was like unto Elijah, so am I as Elisha, and his place was but as Gehazi, and could stand no longer than my will and pleasure was." Claxton had been formally blessed, therefore he could never be damned, but excommunicated he could be and was. He at once dropt out and we hear of him no more.

The second revolt was much more serious. "There were four conspirators in the rebellion . . . for which I damned two of them, and the other two I did excommunicate." This time the fomenter of discord was a busy Scotchman. Muggleton calls him Walter Bohenan, which appears to be only a *phonetic* representation of Walter *Buchanan*. That so sagacious a seer as Muggleton should have been betrayed into associating himself intimately with a canny Scot is truly wonderful, and illustrates the eternal verity that "we are all of us weak at times," even the prophets. *Bohenan's* self-assertion led him on to dizzy heights of towering presumption, until at last "he acted the highest act of rebellion that ever was acted." It was all in vain ; he was cut off for ever — perished from the congregation; utterly damned, and thereupon disappears, swallowed up of darkness and silence.

Muggleton lived twenty-six years after this last revolt, exercising unquestioned authority ; an autocratic prophet to whom something like worship was offered even to the last.   He was far advanced in his eighty-ninth year when he died.   He was far on towards seventy when he was brought before Jeffreys, then Common Serjeant, and other justices, on a charge of blasphemy.   Jeffreys was as yet a novice in those arts of which he became the acknowledged master a few years after, but already he quite equalled his future self in his savage brutality to the poor monomaniac.   "He was a man," says Muggleton, "whose voice was very loud ; but he is one of the worst devils in nature."   The jury hesitated to bring in their verdict, knowing well enough what would follow, but Jeffrey's look and manner cowed them.   The prophet was condemned to pay a fine of £500, to stand in the pillory three times for two hours *without the usual protection to his head*, which those condemned to such a barbarous punishment were allowed.   He was to have his books burned by the common hangman, and to remain in Newgate till his fine was paid.   Only a man of an iron constitution could have come out of the ordeal with his life. Muggleton bore it all ; remained in Newgate for a year, compounded for his fine in the sum of £100, which his friends advanced, and was a free man on the 19th of July, 1677, a day which the Muggletonians observed as the prophet's Hegira.

As early as 1666 he had many followers on the Continent, and in that year the *Transcendant Spiritual Treatise* was translated into German by a convert who came over to London to confer with the sage. Except on very rare occasions he never left London, nor indeed the parish in which he was born. He pursued the trade of a tailor till late in life, but his books had sold largely, and he managed to get together a competence, and was at one time worried by his neighbours and fined for refusing to serve in some parish offices. There was a fund of sagacity about the man which appears frequently in his later letters, but an utter absence of all sentiment and all sympathy. He had no *nerves*. Staid, stern, and curiously insensible to physical pain, he was absolutely fearless, with a constitution that could defy any hardships and bear any strain upon it.

When we come to the *teaching* of Muggleton, we find ourselves in a tangled maze of nonsense far too inconsequential to allow of any intelligible account being given of it. Jacob Boehm's mistiest dreams are clearness itself compared with the English prophet's utterances. Others might talk of the divine cause or the divine power or the divine person, " fumbling exceedingly " and falling back in an intellectual swoon upon the stony bosom of the Unknowable. Muggleton grimly told you that there was a personal Trinity in the universe—God, man and devil—and each had his body. If you pressed him for further particulars he poured forth words that might mean anything, a metallic jargon which you were ordered to receive and ponder. Such as it was, however, you had to accept or reject it at your peril. Why should an inspired prophet argue?

Something must be set down to the circumstances in which he found himself, and to the dreadfully chaotic condition which the moral sentiments and religious beliefs of the multitude had been reduced to during the wild anarchy of the seventeenth century. There were two men in England who were *quite certain*—George Fox was one, Muggleton was the other. Everybody else was doubting, hesitating, groping for the light, moaning at the darkness. These two men *knew*, other people were seeking to know. George Fox went forth to win the world over from darkness to light. Muggleton stayed at home, he *was* the light. They that wanted it must come to him to find it. All through England there was clamour and hubbub of many voices, men going to and fro, always on the move, trying experiments of all kinds. Here was one man, " a still strong man in a blatant land," who was calm, steadfast, unmovable, and always at home. He did not want you, whoever you were; he was perfectly indifferent to you and your concerns. Preach? No! he never preached, he never cared to speak till he was spoken to. If you went to him as an oracle, then he spake as a god.

Moreover, when the Restoration came and the high pressure that had been kept up in some states of society was suddenly taken off, there was a frantic rage for pleasure, which included the wildest debauchery and the most idiotic attempts at amusement. Then, too, the haste to be rich agitated the minds of all classes; Westward ho! was the cry not only of Pilgrim Fathers but of reckless adventurers of all kinds. From across the sea came the ships of Tarshish bringing gold, and silver, and ivory, and apes, and peacocks, and a thousand tales of El Dorado. Muggleton the prophet, with that lank brown hair of his and the dreamy eye and the resolute lips, waited unmoved. Pleasure? If he wondered at anything it was to know what meaning there could be in the word. Riches? What purpose could they serve? To him it seemed that the Decalogue contained one wholly superfluous enactment; why should men covet? There would have been some reason in limiting the number of the commandments to nine; nine is the product of three times three. Think of that! This man in that wicked age must have appeared to many a standing

miracle, if only for this reason, that he was the one
man in London who was content, passing his days in
a stubborn rapture, as little inclined for play or
laughter as the sphinx in the desert, which the sand
storms can beat against but never stir.

So far from Muggleton's influence and authority
growing less as he grew older, it went on steadily
increasing; there was a mystery and an awe that
gathered round him, and latterly he was regarded
rather as an inspired oracle than as a seer. The
voice of prophecy ceased; he had left his words on
record for all future ages, but from day to day his
advice was asked, and people soon found it was
worth listening to. In the latter years of his life his
letters dealt with the ordinary affairs of men.
People wrote to inquire about their matrimonial
affairs, their quarrels, their business difficulties,
whether they must conform to this or that enactment of the State, how they might outwit the per-
secutors and skulk behind the law. Muggleton
replies with surprising shrewdness and good sense,
and now and then exhibits a familiarity with the
quips and quirks of the law that he can only have
acquired by the necessity which suffering had laid
upon him. His language is always rugged, for he
had received little or no education; he is very unsafe
in his grammar, but he has a plain, homely vocabu-

lary, forcible and copious, which, like most mystics, he was compelled to enrich on occasion, and which he does not scruple to enrich in his own way. His style certainly improves as he gets older, and in these letters one meets now and then with passages that are almost melodious, the sentences following one another in a kind of plaintive rhythm, and sounding as you read them aloud, like a Gregorian chant. He died of natural decay, the machine worn out. His last words were, "Now hath God sent death unto me." They laid him on his bed, and he slept and woke not. Nearly 250 of the faithful followed him to his grave. It is clear that the sect had not lost ground as time moved on.

Not the least feature in this curious chapter of religious history is that the Muggletonians should have survived as a sect to our own days. As late as 1846 an elaborate index to the Muggletonian writings was issued, and the *Divine Songs of the Muggletonians*, written exclusively by believers, show that there has been a strange continuity of composition among them, and that, too, such composition as ordinary mortals have never known the like of. Yet Muggleton never broke forth into verse. Joanna Southcott could not keep down her impulse to pour forth her soul in metre; Muggleton is never excited, the emotional had no charm for him. So, too, he never cared for music, he makes no allusion to it Nay, he speaks slightingly of worship, of prayer and praise, especially of congregational worship. It was allowable to the little men, a concession to the weak which the strong in the faith might be expected to dispense with sooner or later. For himself, isolated and self-contained, he could do without the aids to faith which the multitude ask for and find support in. He held himself aloof; he had no sympathy to offer, he asked for none; nay, he did not even need his followers, he could do without them. The question for them was, Could they do without him? For more than two centuries they have kept on vehemently answering No!

Of late years a class of specialists has risen up among us who have treated us to quite a new philosophy—to wit, the philosophy of religion. To these thinkers I leave the construction of theories on Muggleton's place in the history of religion or philosophy; to them, too, I leave the question of what was the secret of his success and power. Much more interesting to me is the problem how the sect has gone on retaining its vitality. Perhaps the great secret of that permanence has been that Muggleton did not give his followers too much to believe or too much to do. He disdained details, he was never precise and meddlesome. If the Muggle-

tonians wished to pray, let them; to sing, there was
no objection; to meet together in their conventicles,
it was a harmless diversion. But they must manage
these things themselves, and provide for difficulties
as they arose. It was no part of the prophet's office
to make bye-laws which might require to be altered
any day. Thus it came about that the sect was left
at Muggleton's death absolutely unfettered by any
petty restraints upon its freedom of development.
The believers must manage their own affairs. There
is one God and Muggleton is His prophet—that was
really the sum and substance of their creed. That
followed on a small scale which is observable on a
large scale among the Moslems, the prophet's
followers found themselves more and more thrown
back upon their prophet till he became almost an
object of adoration. The creed of Islam without
Mahomet would be to millions almost inconceivable;
the Muggletonian God without Muggleton would not
be known

Says her Royal Highness, looking over my shoulder, "You have written quite enough about those crazy, vulgar people. It's all old world talk. There are no prophets now; there never will be any more."

No more prophets! The *prophetical succession* never stops, never will stop. When Muggleton died Emanuel Swedenborg was a boy of ten; twenty years afterwards the new prophet was walking about London just as the old one had done, living the same lonely life, conversing with the angels and writing of heaven and hell and conjugal love, and— well, a great deal else besides; and, odd coincidence, it was in that same Eastcheap where Muggleton had damned the Quakers in 1653 that the Swedenborgians held their first assembly in 1788, just about the same time that Joanna Southcott came to London, and before Joseph Smith and Brigham Young were born or thought of. No, no. The prophets are not improved off the face of the earth. They never will be. They will turn up again and again. You can no more hope to exterminate them by culture than you can hope to produce them by machinery. *Propheta nascitur non fit.* For once her Royal Highness was wrong.

171

PRINTED IN GREAT BRITAIN BY RICHARD CLAY & SONS, LIMITED, BUNGAY, SUFFOLK.

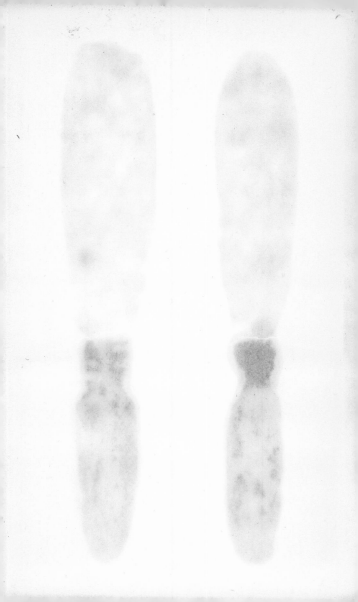

DATE DUE

GAYLORD

PRINTED IN U.S.A.